LIFE SKILLS FOR TEENAGE GIRLS

HOW TO BUILD SELF-ESTEEM & INDEPENDENCE, AVOID DRAMA, FIND A JOB, STAY HEALTHY, BUY YOUR FIRST CAR, COOK, CLEAN AND EVERYTHING IN BETWEEN

GRACE DANIELS

© Copyright 2023 - Okanagan Lifelong Learning Press. All rights reserved.

It is not legal to reproduce, duplicate, or transmit any part of this document in either electronic means or in printed format. Recording of this publication is strictly prohibited and any storage of this document is not allowed unless with written permission from the publisher except for the use of brief quotations in a book review.

This book is a work of fiction. Any resemblance to persons, living or dead, or places, events or locations is purely coincidental.

All rights reserved. This book or any portion thereof may not be reproduced or used in any manner whatsoever without the express written permission of the publisher except for the use of brief quotations in a book review.

First edition, 2023.

ALSO BY GRACE DANIELS

Life Skills for Kids

Life Skills for Teenage Boys

Coming Soon:

The Growth Mindset for Teens

The Growth Mindset for Kids

CONTENTS

Introduction	ix
1. TIPS TO BUILD SELF-CONFIDENCE	1
Journaling tips	2
Positivity From the Inside Out	2
Positive Words	4
Tips to Improve Self-Esteem	5
2. PEER PRESSURE AND FRIEND STRUGGLES	8
What is Peer Pressure?	9
Tips for Handling Peer Pressure	10
Friendships, Fights, and Communication	12
Calming Down During Fights	13
3. SOCIAL SKILLS	16
The Importance of Social Skills	17
Important Social Skills	17
Quick Tips for Making More Friends	22
4. A GUIDE TO EMOTIONS AND MENTAL HEALTH	25
The Five Primary Emotions	25
A Guide to Processing Your Emotions— Emotional Regulation	29
Learning How to Sit With Your Emotions— Steps to Follow	33
How Bad Mental Health Affects You	34
The Basics of Good Mental Health	35
5. BODY IMAGE	37
What is Body Dysmorphia?	38
What are Body Positivity and Body Neutrality?	39
Tips to Improve Body Image	40
6. HAIR AND SKINCARE— IT MATTERS!	43
Embracing Your Natural Hair	43
Hair Maintenance Tips	45
Skincare Tips	46
7. FINDING YOUR STYLE	48
Styling Tips	48
Finding Your Body Type— Styles that Suit You	50

A Guide to Accessories	52
Different Aesthetics to Try Out	53
8. MAINTAINING YOUR PHYSICAL HEALTH AND HYGIENE	**56**
A Balanced Lifestyle	56
Feminine Hygiene Quick Tips	58
A Guide to Periods	59
Eating Enough	61
9. FIRST AID SKILLS	**66**
Rules to Remember Before Giving First Aid	66
Creating and Keeping a First Aid Kit	67
Different Ailments and How to Treat Them in an Emergency	68
When do I call first responders?	72
10. SMART MONEY	**73**
Budgeting 101	73
Tips to Save More	76
Tips for managing loans	79
11. A GUIDE TO YOUR FIRST CAR	**81**
Quick Tips For Buying Your First Car	81
Loans and the Purchasing Process	83
Basic Automotive Skills	84
12. SAFETY SKILLS AND SELF-DEFENSE	**88**
Basic Street Safety Tips	88
Internet Safety Tips	93
Safe Partying	95
Personal Boundaries	97
13. GOAL-SETTING AND TIME MANAGEMENT	**100**
Setting Reachable Goals	100
Time Management Tips	102
14. ORGANIZATIONAL SKILLS	**108**
Start decluttering	110
Designated places	111
Go one area at a time— learning to divide and conquer	111
15. GETTING A JOB AND KEEPING IT	**113**
Tips to Prepare to Get Your First Job	113
Now It's Time to Work Hard	117
16. PRACTICAL HOME SKILLS	**120**
Managing a Home— Domestic Skills	120
Cooking and Food	123

17. PROBLEM-SOLVING SKILLS ... 127
    What are Problem-Solving Skills? ... 127
    Six Steps to Solving a Problem ... 128
    The Enemies of Problem-Solving Skills ... 131
    Exercises to Increase Problem-Solving Skills ... 132

18. FINDING A SENSE OF INDEPENDENCE AND DEVELOPING
    YOURSELF ... 134
    Finding Independence ... 134
    Keys to Self-Development ... 137

    Final Words ... 139
    Also by Grace Daniels ... 141
    References ... 143

INTRODUCTION

Being a teenager is complicated— you're getting older, becoming your own person, making new friends, and planning for the future—and the ever-changing nature of your teenage years can be hard. It's even more annoying that school doesn't teach you everything you need to know before you're thrown into the "real world." Friendships can be stressful, body image can be a struggle, and don't even get started thinking about money.

Fret not! This book is here to help. Any questions you may have about peer pressure, organization, skincare, self-esteem, or any other life skill will be answered! You are entering a new phase of life where you need to be more independent and have the skills to gain confidence.

While the internet has a lot of information on how to navigate your teens, it can be overwhelming, contradictory, and unhelpful at times. But with the basic skills and exercises outlined in this guidebook, you will be able to figure it all out yourself and at your own pace!

Whenever you have a question about something specific, or a new problem arises, simply flip through to the right chapter and get to reading.

Let's jump right in!

CHAPTER 1
TIPS TO BUILD SELF-CONFIDENCE

Low self-esteem is something everyone struggles with from time to time. But *self-esteem* is just a word that is used to describe how you feel about yourself. It can also mean high or low confidence. If you struggle with this it means you may think bad things about yourself and aren't happy with who you are. But high self-esteem means the opposite.

If you have low self-esteem you might find yourself thinking that you aren't good enough, being too hard on yourself, or feeling bad about yourself. All of these things work to make your self-esteem even worse over time.

But people with high self-esteem feel accepted and loved, are proud of what they can do, believe in themselves, and see their value. When you are more confident in yourself and believe that you can do hard things, you will be able to make more friends and live a happier life.

Self-esteem is something that doesn't really begin with you, it starts as a child with the adults around you. The people you look up to have a big influence on how you feel about yourself. That little voice in your head will repeat the things people said to you throughout your childhood.

Having low self-esteem isn't all about feeling bad about yourself, it can actually lead to a lot of other consequences. You might find yourself having a hard time making new friends, having a difficult time in school, and feeling lonely, stressed, or anxious.

JOURNALING TIPS

Keeping a journal is powerful. If you get into the habit of reflecting on your day, expressing what is on your mind, and reliving positive moments you will naturally become more reflective and positive. You don't need to do this every single day, in fact, you can start by scheduling in weekly journaling and self-awareness time. Here are a few ways you can get started on your journaling journey:

- Write out at least three things you are grateful for each day or week.
- Use any of the reflective journaling prompts in this book!
- Use the first page to simply write about yourself. Talk about your interests, friends, favorite TV shows, outfits, family, and current life situations.
- Use it as a safe space where you can talk about all of your emotions and thoughts without judgment.
- Journal about your future plans, dreams, and aspirations.
- Process problems and analyze situations that you are trying to figure out.
- Set goals and make plans for what you will do to reach them.

POSITIVITY FROM THE INSIDE OUT

In order to increase your self-esteem and become more confident, you should start to focus on the positives in life. This sounds a lot easier than it is, but you should do this if you want to start feeling better about yourself. Creating positivity starts with getting rid of negativity.

Here's something you can start doing with your negative thoughts:

You might tell yourself that you are "too stupid" if you get one bad grade or get an answer wrong on a test. But this is not true, and deep down you know this. So, start trying to note down the negative thoughts you have throughout the day in your diary or journal.

When you see the list of these thoughts it can feel pretty bad. But now, instead of looking at all of these bad things you think about yourself, look at them with positivity. So, follow these steps to fight off the negative thoughts you wrote down:

1. Ask yourself: When did I start thinking these things?

Noticing that these thoughts did not come from you, or that someone else influenced them means that they *aren't true!*

2. Write down any evidence you have for your negative thoughts. (Not just one bad test, because that doesn't count).

You will begin to find that you really don't have any evidence to prove these bad things you think about yourself.

3. Write down three positive things you like about yourself for each negative point you have written down.

Now that you have real proof that these negative thoughts are not true, write them down again on a separate piece of paper. This time, take that paper and destroy it. Either tear it up, cut it up, shred it, or crumple it and put it in the trash. Whatever you do, get rid of it!

From here, make a list of all of the positive things you think about yourself. These can be physical things you like about yourself, personality traits, or even positive things people say about you. Whenever you begin to think negative thoughts about yourself again, you now have a list of all the amazing things about yourself to remind you of positivity!

> **The Benefits of Positivity:**
>
> Positivity doesn't just feel good... there are some REAL benefits to thinking more positively! These include:
>
> - Living a longer life!
> - Less risk of sicknesses
> - Lower levels of anxiety and depression
> - Thinking more creatively
> - Better leadership skills

POSITIVE WORDS

The words you tell yourself are just as important as the things you think about yourself. If you get into the habit of encouraging yourself with your words, out loud, every day, you will begin to believe them about yourself. Practicing saying kind things to your own face in the mirror is a great exercise to start thinking more positively. You can create a list of your favorite things about yourself and stick them to your mirror, or say them out loud! Below are some examples you can use to start:

"I am an amazing person"

"Today is going to be an awesome day."

"I am important."

"I am beautiful inside and out."

"I am smart."

"I can do what I put my mind to."

"Today I am going to shine."

"I am unique and special."

"Nothing is impossible for me."

"I am strong and independent."

"Today is my day."

"I am confident."

"I am loved and happy."

"I can do hard things."

TIPS TO IMPROVE SELF-ESTEEM

Positive thinking and the positive words exercise above can really help with improving self-esteem! But when you are going about your daily life there are even more tricks you can use to gain confidence in yourself and become unstoppable.

Here are some awesome ways you can become more confident and improve your self-esteem:

Accept that you are not perfect— This can be hard, especially when your parents and teachers seem to expect perfection from you. But you are human, and you are never going to be perfect. If you are able to let go of the belief that you can't make mistakes your confidence will increase! This can be hard, but try starting with accepting your imperfections rather than getting sad and disappointed about them.

Journal about the good parts of your day— Learning how to practice gratitude and pointing out the good parts of each day can help you remember the positives more often. This practice will help you focus on the happy moments of your day, and the good things about yourself. Celebrate your wins!

Pick up a new hobby— Try something you've always wanted to do! This is a great way of boosting confidence and proving to yourself that you are capable of new and challenging things. Starting something new, meeting new people, and accomplishing hard things will make you so proud of yourself!

Celebrate every little win— Every time you do something cool, celebrate it! These celebrations don't need to be big, and the task doesn't need to be too challenging. But when you get in the habit of telling yourself that you deserve a celebration, you will grow your confidence.

Stop the self-comparison— It is so easy to look at the people around you and want what they have, thinking that you aren't enough, or that you don't have enough. But self-comparison is the biggest killer of self-esteem. If you want to become more confident here are a few ways you can stop self-comparison:

- Limit your time on social media. The standards of women and money on social media platforms are completely unrealistic. They only make us feel bad about ourselves. It's best to limit time on social media and be sure you are aware of when you start comparing yourself to the people there.
- Practice thankfulness for what you already have and what you can do.
- Remind yourself daily of your unique and beautiful self!
- Focus on what you have already accomplished and what your personal strengths are!

Journals are a great way to begin processing your emotions. When you are able to express what you are feeling you will be able to better understand yourself and your experiences. So, if you don't have a journal or a diary already, I highly recommend that you pick one up, even if you are just using the prompts from this book.

At the end of every chapter, we will have some questions and prompts you can journal about to think deeper about what you discovered. You don't need to do every prompt at once, just come back here whenever you feel you need a little more support!

CHAPTER 2
PEER PRESSURE AND FRIEND STRUGGLES

"Peer" is just another word for the people around you who are a similar age and have similar experiences, activities, communities, and interests. Your peers don't have to actually be your friends, but they can still have a large influence on you and your actions. It can be hard when you want to look cool and not embarrass yourself in front of friends, or even people you don't know very well. That is where peer pressure comes from.

Friend struggles are also another hard part of being a teen. Conflicts and fights will happen, but it's up to you to find ways to resolve them with compassion. Learning how to talk to your friends, set boundaries, and handle conflicts is an essential part of growing up. In this chapter, we will talk about how to combat negative peer pressure, speak your mind, solve friend problems, and have healthier friendships!

> **Questions and Prompts for Your Personal Diary**
>
> 1. On a scale of one to ten (one being the lowest), how high is your self-esteem?
> 2. Do you often find yourself comparing your body, skills, or ideas to the people around you?
> 3. If you struggle with a comparison, what do you compare about yourself most often?
> 4. What is one thing you are going to start doing this week to increase your self-esteem?
> 5. What is a positive sentence (or affirmation) you are going to start saying in the mirror every day?

You are in control, and it's time for you to start recognizing your self-worth. It can be hard to learn how to be confident as a teenager, but it is possible! In the next chapter, you will learn all about how to navigate and respond to friendship struggles and peer pressure.

WHAT IS PEER PRESSURE?

Peer pressure can be either positive or negative. When it is positive, the people around you will help push you to be the best version of yourself. But negative peer pressure happens when a friend (or peer) forces you to do or participate in something in order to feel accepted, even if you don't want to (*How to handle peer pressure,* 2023).

When people talk about peer pressure, most of the time they're talking about the negative kind. When you experience negative peer pressure it can make you feel like you don't belong, guilty, or disappointed that you acted in a way you disagree with.

> **Examples of what *negative* peer pressure can lead to:**
>
> Feeling the need to dress in a specific way to fit in.
>
> Letting peers copy your work, or copying someone else's school work.
>
> Being cyberbullied, bullied, or participating in bullying of any kind.
>
> Stealing or shoplifting due to outside pressure.
>
> Posting unrealistic images (filtered) on social media.
>
> Trying unhealthy new things, such as smoking.
>
> Drinking alcohol or using drugs.
>
> Poor body image and eating habits.
>
> Lying to trusted adults.
>
> Not participating in activities you used to enjoy.
>
> Excluding certain people from a friend group or specific activities.
>
> Feeling the need to act in a certain way around a group of peers.

Peer pressure can come from school, friends, or even social media. It sucks, and it can lead to feeling more uncomfortable in your skin, distancing yourself from friends and family, and lowering your self-esteem and confidence. The good news is that there are things you can do to prevent yourself from being negatively impacted by your peers!

TIPS FOR HANDLING PEER PRESSURE

Plan ahead — If you are realizing that you have experienced peer pressure in the past, it's time to start planning ahead for when it happens again. Before you head out with a group of peers, especially ones you know may pressure you, plan out what you are going to say to them. Being prepared can help you feel more confident when saying "no" to certain things.

Paying attention to how you feel — You need to listen to yourself and how you are feeling if you want to stay true to your beliefs. This all starts with listening to your intuition. If you start to feel unsafe or uncomfortable i could be a sign that things are off and that you should get out of the situation.

Have a secret code with your parents or other trusted adults— Confiding in the trusted adults around you can be a great way to keep yourself out of situations you don't want to be a part of. Try to create a secret code with your parents or someone you trust. Then they can call you and say that you need to come home or that an emergency happened. This way you can escape a situation without having to confront the people around you.

Prepare an excuse— If you know that you might be entering a situation where your friends may pressure you, create an excuse beforehand. It can be hard to voice disagreement in a group, so an excuse can be more comfortable. This is similar to the "planning ahead" tip but goes a step further. Some examples can be found below:

If your friends will be smoking, and you don't want to:	"I have a sore throat," or "I'm not feeling good, the smoke will make me sicker."
If you might be pressured into stealing:	"I don't even like that, it's kind of ugly," or "I already have that at home."
If you will be pressured into drinking:	"I have plans tomorrow and need to be up early," or "Someone needs to drive, I'll be the designated driver."
If you feel pressured to wear certain clothes:	"That's not my style," or "It doesn't feel comfortable on me."

Some signs you or your friends may be struggling with peer pressure include:

CHANGING THE WAY THEY TALK

CHOOSING THE SAME STYLE

NOT WORKING AS HARD AT SCHOOL

Seek out positive friendships— The absolute best way to avoid peer pressure in most cases is to make friends who will not pressure you to do things you don't want to, or who will be positive influences on you. It can be easier to say "no" to something a group is doing if you have friends saying the same thing.

Don't make it a big deal— It doesn't need to be a big confrontation, and you can still hang around the people who might be pressuring things. But you can say "no," change the topic, and move on with your time.

Making mistakes and learning from them— If you do give in and do something because of your peers and regret it, you can still learn from your experiences. Use your mistakes as learning experiences to find where things went wrong and how you can escape these situations in the future. This is a big part of learning how to be independent. You are going to make mistakes along the way. The important thing is what you do with these mistakes.

FRIENDSHIPS, FIGHTS, AND COMMUNICATION

No matter how nice your friends are, there will always be conflicts. You can either let little fights ruin your friendship, or you can learn to resolve fights and move forward. The first step in making good friendships and ending conflicts is effective communication. This means listening, not just talking. Here are ten tips on how you can bring up issues with your friends and hear their side of the story:

1. Listen before you speak— Be sure to hear what the other person has to say before you go on. Make an effort to listen and deeply consider their point of view and experiences.
2. Stay focused on the conflict that is happening at the moment, and don't bring up old fights or past arguments.
3. Make sure the other person is in a place to listen to you in that moment, and not distracted or unwilling to listen. Communication takes both people to work.
4. Don't interrupt. You wouldn't want the other person to interrupt you, so don't do that to them… that's just basic respect.
5. Try to recognize the emotions that the other person is feeling. When you are able to see that they are sad, angry, or frustrated you will be able to understand them more.
6. Keep it clear, think about your words before you say them, and be sure that they make sense.
7. Listen to yourself as you speak. Don't raise your voice and get angry too quickly. Staying calm and aware will make these conversations much smoother.
8. Stop playing the blame game. If you accuse someone the whole time they will not want to listen to you or work with you.
9. Ask questions to get a better understanding of the other person's side of the story.
10. Lastly, be willing and ready to accept your differences, forgive, and move on.

CALMING DOWN DURING FIGHTS

It can be hard to keep your cool when you are having a fight, disagreement, or conflict with a friend. But if you are able to calm yourself down, solving problems will be *so* much easier! We all get angry, and it's okay to be mad, just don't let your emotions take control and make you do things you might regret. Saying mean things and acting on your anger can make you lose friends, but the goal is to solve these problems... So here are some steps to calm yourself down in the middle of a fight or disagreement with a friend:

An Awesome Breathing Exercise

If you are taking a quick break away from the other person or need to calm yourself down in the middle of an argument, breathing exercises can be extremely helpful. The breathing exercise below can be done at any time, anywhere:

1. Fill your belly with each breath you take, imagining the fresh air washing through your whole body.
2. After a few deep breaths, start inhaling through your nose and out through your mouth.
3. Now, start counting to five with each inhale, letting it flow out after. This will allow your mind to fully focus on calming down rather than the emotions you are feeling.
4. Repeat as many times as you need.

Other tips to resolve conflicts:

Take a break— Things can get heated in arguments really quickly. Sometimes this means you can't figure out the conflict right away. If you find yourself getting too angry, raising your voice, or saying rude things, it might be time to excuse yourself and take a break for a few minutes. This will give you time to think about the issues and get away from the intense fighting.

Properly communicating your point of view— When you are explaining yourself to someone it is important to remember a few things. You want your friend to listen to you, and you want them to understand you. Keep these things in mind when expressing yourself:

- Speak slowly— Let yourself think and process as you speak so you don't say anything you don't really mean.
- Look them in the eyes so they know you care.
- Speak with "I" language, not "you" language— This simply means that you are not going to place all of the blame on your friend. Instead, you should talk about how you feel, what you are experiencing, and what you need.

Make a plan together— You are two people, and both of you are going to need to work out your issues together. Below are some steps you can take to work out a fight with a friend *together:*

1. Step away and choose not to come back together until you have both calmed down.
2. Choose a space to talk where you both feel comfortable.
3. Try to see the other person's point of view, not just your own.
4. Try to keep things as positive as possible. And keep yourself from being aggressive or critical.

Questions and Prompts for Your Personal Diary

1. Have you ever experienced negative peer pressure?

    If so, what was your experience?
2. How did you feel when you participated in something you didn't want to?
3. What emotions did you feel the last time you got into an argument with a friend?
4. What happened in the conflict? Do you think it was handled in a healthy way?

Dealing with peer pressure and conflicts with friends can be hard, but it is not impossible. When you have the skills listed in this chapter you will realize that you can stand your ground, still make friends, and resolve even the worst fights. However, there are still more important social skills that you are going to need to learn in order to develop yourself as a teenager. The skills in the next chapter will help you with friends, jobs, school, and how to respectfully speak with other adults in your life!

CHAPTER 3
SOCIAL SKILLS

Social skills are the different skills we use to interact and communicate with the people around us. They are both verbal (using words and tone of voice) and non-verbal (body language and physical appearance). Humans are naturally very social, and throughout the centuries we have created specific ways to effectively communicate with one another (*Skills You Need*, 2023).

Some people seem to naturally be good at talking to people and connecting with others, but the reality is that *anyone* can discover those same skills. It's all a matter of figuring out the basics and using them frequently.

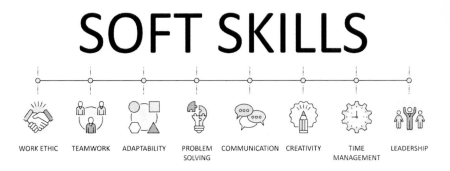

THE IMPORTANCE OF SOCIAL SKILLS

There are a lot of benefits to developing your social skills, some of which include the following:

- Better relationships (and more of them).
- Increased communication skills, and being understood better— with both peers *and* adults in your life.
- Generally increased positivity and happiness!
- Better teamwork and cooperation skills.
- Being better at handling and expressing your emotions.
- Greater success in school.
- Developing better self-awareness.
- Fewer chances of experiencing bullying.
- Increased job opportunities and success.

IMPORTANT SOCIAL SKILLS

There are many different ways to engage in conversations and develop proper social skills. In this chapter, we will go over the top nine most important social skills, how to learn them, and how they help in daily life.

1. Making eye contact

Making and holding proper eye contact is likely one of the most important non-verbal social skills out there. However, it is a well-known fact that teenagers avoid eye contact like the plague, especially with authority figures. There are a lot of reasons for this— some examples are being shy, being on phones, not being in a great mood, or having low self-esteem. It can be difficult, and even anxiety-provoking, but proper eye contact shows you are engaged in a conversation, that you respect the other person, and that you care. Here are some general eye-contact tips to help you develop this skill (Reynolds, 2020):

- Don't look the other person directly in the eyes if that's too daunting for you, instead look at the bridge of their nose between their eyes.
- Try holding eye contact for five to ten seconds at a time. Then, look off somewhere else for a few seconds before repeating.

- When you look to the side or break eye contact, try to slowly move your eyes. Quickly looking away too often can make you seem anxious, shy, and generally uncomfortable.
- Try out the 50/70 rule. In a conversation try to make eye contact 50 percent of the time when you are listening, and when you're the one talking try to keep eye contact 70 percent of the time. You don't need to get super technical about this, it's just a good guideline to keep in mind.

2. Addressing people properly

Addressing people by name is a sign of respect and care. It is common practice to address your friends with a "what's up girlfriend!" But as you are getting older, the social game requires a little more formality. It might not sound fun, but it will make people remember you, your respect, and that you are well-spoken.

Someone's name is their unique identity, their title is something to be acknowledged, and it's all about using the right names at the right time. By addressing someone individually and properly you will automatically make a great introduction. Here are some examples of how to switch up what you call people:

Professors and teachers— NOT their first name, but rather their title and last name.

Parents of your friends— If you don't know them well, their title (Mr. or Mrs.) and their last name are respectful.

A new friend or acquaintance— Their first name is respectful, not "girl," "bestie," or other informal nicknames.

3. The power of introductions

As mentioned above, names and properly addressing the people around you are really important pieces of good introductions. But simple and casual introductions (like: "So, yeah... this is Amanda" or "Hi, uh, I'm .") aren't going to cut it. Learning proper introductions can be daunting, and many people overcomplicate them... or avoid them all together.

Making good introductions are actually super simple. If you address the person you want to speak to first, then regard the person you are introducing, you have a good introduction. Here are a few examples of how you can do this:

"Hi mom, I would like you to meet my friend, Amanda Jones."

"Hi Dr. Smith, I would like to introduce myself, my name is __."

"Amanda, this is my grandma, Mrs. Smith."

4. Making good first impressions

People make judgments about you and come to conclusions about who you are within five seconds of meeting you. This means that the first five seconds of your first impressions are the most important. Avoid eye contact, slouch a little, or have something in your teeth and people will already have opinions about you based on your appearance and the way you hold yourself. It is extremely hard to reverse a bad first impression. While these might not matter much with your current school friends, they definitely matter when you head off to college and start applying for jobs. Here are some quick tips for making good first impressions:

- Dress for the occasion— The hoodie and sneakers you wear out with your friends will not be appropriate for a job interview, meeting your boyfriend's parents, or going to a nice dinner.
- Keep good posture— Hunching over will make you seem insecure and unsure of yourself… again *first five seconds!*
- Keep up that eye contact we just talked about!
- Smile genuinely, a nice smile goes a long way.
- Be yourself, and avoid being fake. People want to get to know the real you… not a fake version of you.

5. Encouraging others

Being kind and encouraging to the people around you is another great social skill that will help you get far in life. This helps to build the self-esteem of others and deepen relationships. People will also see you with more respect. You can encourage the people around you in many different ways, including (but not limited to): telling people you appreciate them, offering *wanted* advice, writing kind notes, and sharing in their excitement when they succeed.

6. Active listening skills

Hearing and actively listening are not the same thing. Showing people that you are listening to what they are saying to you is a critical social skill. It shows people you respect them, that they deserve to be heard, and that you value the relationship. Active listening is about *showing* you are listening and uses non-verbal body language. Here are some steps you can take to make sure you are actively listening:

- Make eye contact and face the other person with your whole body.
- Pay attention to the body language of the other person and reflect similarly. This might be a smile, relaxed posture, or even hands on their hips.
- Don't interrupt.
- Don't start preparing what you are going to say next. This will distract you and stop you from actually listening to the person you are talking to.

- Show that you are listening with body language and verbal cues. This might look like nodding or shaking your head, saying "I agree," or laughing along.

12 ACTIVE LISTENING SKILLS

PAY ATTENTION

DON'T INTERRUPT

SUMMARIZE

MAINTAIN EYE CONTACT

SHOW INTEREST

REQUEST CLARIFICATION

USE POSITIVE BODY LANGUAGE

PARAPHRASE

WITHHOLD JUDGEMENT

SHOW EMPATHY

REPEAT KEY PHRASES

SHARE

7. Interacting with adults vs. with other teens

Other than talking to your parents and teachers, talking to adults might be a foreign concept for you. When developing your social skills you need to remember that talking to other teens is not the same as talking to adults. However, your teenage years are supposed to prepare you for adulthood. When you get thrown into the "real world" you'll need to be able to have adult conversations with adults. So here are some ways you can get more comfortable with talking to adults:

- Practice makes perfect— talk to family members, stay at the dinner table with your parents' friends, and just try to put yourself out there.
- Practice all of the tips above for eye contact, active listening, and introductions.
- Be curious and ask questions— An easy way to bridge the gap between you and the adults in your life (in a natural way) is by asking questions to initiate conversations.

8. Reading body language

Experts estimate that 70 to 93 percent of our communication is nonverbal (Spence, 2021). Nonverbal communication just means body language and facial expressions. These things speak volumes about how you feel, if you are listening, if someone likes you, and how comfortable others feel around you. Your body does a lot of the talking for you. This means that you can work to avoid awkward conversations and moments by becoming a master of body language. Below are a few forms of body language you can learn to gain an understanding of how you present yourself and how others feel around you:

> **A Guide to Basic Body Language**
>
> *Folded arms*— This generally means someone is closed off or uncomfortable talking about a topic.
>
> *Fidgeting*— This often means someone is nervous or uncomfortable.
>
> *Slouched posture*— This means someone is uninterested or bored.
>
> *Darting eyes (rapidly avoiding eye contact)*— This usually means someone is not confident, shy, or even lying.
>
> *Hands on hips*— Generally, this means someone is confident in themselves and comfortable taking up space.

9. Reciprocal conversational skills

Communication is not a one-way street. When someone is speaking, you need to actively listen *and* provide additional interest in the conversation. This is just a part of "reciprocal" or equal conversation skills. When someone asks you how you are, it is better to say "I'm good, how are you?" Rather than simply, "I'm good."

You can increase your conversational skills by practicing asking people the same questions back. Usually, the rule is that you should offer someone the same level of interest they are showing you. If they ask about your day, don' ask about their whole life story. Be a good listener and offer the same politeness they offer you.

QUICK TIPS FOR MAKING MORE FRIENDS

It can be hard to make new friends. Where do you find them? How do you stay in contact? There are so many questions! You might have the sam friends you did when you were in middle school, or maybe you're friends just because you have the same class or you are neighbors.

Being able to make new friends is a great social skill! While a lot of the tips and social skills in the last section will be helpful, here are some more tips for making new friends as a teen:

Go to new activities and events— The best way to meet new people with similar interests is to go to activities, sports, and events that you like! Getting involved and having a good time with new people will be a very natural way of making new and good friends. You could even start by joining another friend who goes to activities that interest you.

Use those listening skills— We have already talked a bit about listening, but making sure people feel heard and important is another great way of making deep, lasting connections. Introduce yourself to new people, ask them about themselves, and really listen. That is when you will find common interests and shared experiences.

Make a visible effort— It's no secret that friendships take effort. So, if you are looking to make and keep more friends, showing them that you are willing to put in the effort is a great way of doing this! Don't wait for other people to arrange an activity or hang out, both parties need to put in the effort to make a friendship work.

Help others— Volunteering with local organizations doing work you are passionate about is another great way of meeting people with similar interests. You can bond with people over causes you care about and have regularly scheduled meet-ups!

Be open with your body language— To attract people and get them to open up you need to show them that you are open and friendly with your body language. Offering a smile, uncrossing your arms, and talking with your hands are great ways to start!

> **Questions and Prompts for Your Personal Diary**
>
> 1. Do you think you need more practice with the social skills we talked about in this chapter? If so, which ones?
> 2. What are your greatest strengths when it comes to social skills?
> 3. When and where do you feel most confident? (Examples: with your parents, in dance class, or maybe with your other friends.)
> 4. Who are your closest friends and how did you meet them?

It's no secret that emotions run high when you're a teenager. But it feels like no one ever shows us what to do with them, how to process them, or what mental health even is. The next chapter is all about emotions and making your mental health a priority!

CHAPTER 4
A GUIDE TO EMOTIONS AND MENTAL HEALTH

Emotions run high for all of us— and will for the rest of our lives. When you are a teenager you will experience a lot of new feelings. You're changing so much during this time, and it can be hard to express what you are going through. This chapter will outline what the five primary emotions are, how you can express them in a healthy way, what emotional regulation is, and all about mental health!

THE FIVE PRIMARY EMOTIONS

The primary emotions are the main five emotions that scientists recognize (Ekman, 2022). These five primary human emotions include happiness, sadness, fear, disgust, and anger. You might think, "That can't be true, I feel a lot more than five!" Just remember that these are simply the *core* emotions that all other feelings come from. Excitement and pride come from happiness, anxiety and embarrassment come from fear, regret flows from sadness, and the list goes on.

The first step in processing your emotions and understanding your mental health is understanding the basics of emotions themselves. When you have a handle on these main categories of emotions you will be able to recognize the big emotions you feel (one of the main five), and then dig deeper.

Happiness

Joy and happiness are positive feelings. Calmness, peace, satisfaction, and excitement are all subcategories of the general feeling of happiness. We generally like to feel calm, joyful, and in a positive mood. Smiling, laughing, and doing something you enjoy will create happiness.

The world around us likes to make us think that tons of money, a new car, social media followers, or a designer bag will make us feel happy. But that's not the reality. The emotion of happiness is something completely unique to you, and outside influences don't affect it very much (such as material items). Even further, genuine happiness has been linked to both mental and physical well-being.

Sadness

The next of the primary emotions is sadness, which is something we all experience on different levels on a regular basis. However, we each experience the depth of the sadness differently, depending on how things affect us. This is an emotion that can often be triggered by a specific experience, memory, or negative thought.

There might be times when you are sad but have no idea why… just that you are sad. If you find yourself experiencing long periods of deep sadness this can turn into depression (which we will discuss in more detail later).

Everyone expresses sadness differently. You might find yourself crying, isolating yourself, seeking solace with friends, or even having trouble sleeping. The root cause of the sadness will make it appear in different forms.

Fear

If your mind or body senses any sort of threat you will experience the feeling of fear. This primary emotion is a core part of being human and is what has helped us survive. Fear can range from crippling anxiety where you can't leave your house to a bit of nervousness before giving a speech… but these are both sensations of fear.

People experience fear in many different ways, just like with any emotion. Different people will experience different triggers, fears, and levels of fear

This emotion causes stress levels to increase and will put you in either fight or flight mode.

Fear can be seen in panic attacks, phobias, self-isolation, social or general anxiety, trauma-based fears, being hyperaware, or not being able to see the world around you clearly.

Disgust

When you see or experience something you find unnatural, unpleasant, or unwanted, your natural reaction will be disgust. It might sound kind of weird that disgust is listed as a primary emotion, however, the feeling of disgust actually works to keep us safe from danger. For example, our bodies are disgusted and turned away by the smell of spoiled food; this then stops us from eating it and getting sick.

Disgust can also be felt towards experiences and people. You might not know why you are turned away from a specific person but you just are. Maybe it's something they said in the past, something they wear, or how they act.

There are many different ways to describe and communicate disgust such as: withdrawing, loathing, dislike, disapproval, hate, offense, disturbance, nauseating, or discomfort.

Anger

Anger is the last of the primary emotions, and it is something that you will experience a lot in your teenage years. You are becoming your own person, developing your own opinions and ideas, and will feel a deeper sense of injustice. This is when conflicts, and therefore anger, occur. When you encounter a threat that makes you angry you may also experience feelings of vulnerability, being trapped, and even a fear of being unable to defend yourself.

Anger can be both a negative and a positive emotion… sounds crazy, right? Anger exists for a reason, and when channeled in the right ways will be the creator of real change. Anger gives us the power to see when something wrong is happening, and gives us the instinct to fight. Anger changes the world.

Feelings of anger can also appear as frustration, annoyance, vengeance, irritation, mad, bitterness, cheating, and insult.

Questions and Prompts for Your Personal Diary— Emotions

1. When do you find yourself experiencing true and deep happiness? Who are you with? Where are you? How does it feel?
2. When is the last time you remember feeling your happiest?
3. Does something specific make you sad on a regular basis?
4. How do you tend to act when you get sad?
5. What is your biggest fear?
6. Have you ever faced a big fear? If so, how did you feel afterward?
7. When was the last time you felt angry? Describe what you did with that emotion… was it good or bad?

A GUIDE TO PROCESSING YOUR EMOTIONS— EMOTIONAL REGULATION

So there are a lot of different emotions, but simply understanding the five primary emotions isn't enough. You are going through a lot of change right now and in the years to come. This means developing into your own person, having mood swings, and experiencing hormonal fluctuations. All of these things piled on top of each other mean *big* emotions.

There is nothing wrong with feeling a lot of emotions, it's just a matter of how you express them. The skill of learning how to properly let out your emotions in appropriate ways is called *emotional regulation*. And that's what this whole section is about.

By discovering how to manage and express your emotions you can:

- Be heard and understood from the beginning because you expressed your thoughts in an appropriate way.
- Get back to feeling like your old self after feeling a strong emotion like deep anger, fear, or sadness.
- Learn to control your reactions and not do things you might regret.
- Identify the emotions other people are feeling.
- Get through awkward situations with ease.
- Soothe yourself in hard times and through big emotional troubles.
- Identify the specific emotions you are feeling.

Before we even talk about how to express and manage your emotions… There are a few things about feelings that you need to keep in mind…

> **Emotions 101**
> 1. Emotions are temporary... They come and go. You will feel so many emotions throughout the day, and none of them will last forever (even if it feels that way).
> 2. There are no *good* or *bad* emotions. But there are healthy and unhealthy ways of expressing emotions and dealing with them.
> 3. The intensity of your emotions will vary. Sometimes they are intense, other times mild. How deeply you feel an emotion will depend on the day and experience... and they will never feel identical.

Talking about your feelings can be hard, and that is why there will be other options later in this chapter. However, in order to discover how to emotionally regulate yourself, respond appropriately in situations, and process these big emotions, there are a few communication skills you will need to learn. Here are the top strategies for emotional expression and regulation you can use to communicate and fill your emotional needs in healthy ways:

1. Find an outlet— Writing, singing, reading, dancing, playing a sport, art, clubs, and exercising are all great ways of channeling your energy into other things and expressing yourself in creative ways.

2. Discover the right words— It can be hard to express an emotion (even if you *want* to) if you don't have the right language to communicate your thoughts properly. Below is a chart of words associated with each of the five primary emotions to get you started on learning the right language to communicate how you feel:

Happiness:	Satisfaction, pride, joy, excitement, peace, calm, humor, contentment, love, amusement, and relief.
Sadness:	Lonely, gloomy, heartbroken, disappointed, grieving, lost, unhappy, hopeless, miserable, depressed, and resigned.
Fear:	Panicked, confused, horrified, doubtful, desperate, anxious, stressed, worried, scared, nervous, and terrified.
Disgust:	Uncomfortable, dislike, aversion, loathing, disapproval, hate, offense, and withdrawal.
Anger:	Irritation, annoyance, injustice, infuriation, insult, vengeance, bitterness, mad, and cheating.

3. Prepare what you need to say— If you have reached a point of wanting to reach out to an adult or simply express your feelings to someone, but are anxious about it, try to plan ahead. Maybe write out some things in your journal that you want to get off your chest, or think about the words you are going to use to properly express yourself.

4. Taking deep breaths when emotions skyrocket— This can be a hard habit to get into, but it's SO worth it! When you begin to feel yourself spiraling, or like your emotions are going from zero to one hundred... stop and take a single breath. This might not do much in the beginning, but getting into a habit of stopping, thinking, and cooling yourself off will make your next actions a lot smarter.

5. Try these journaling prompts— When you can't seem to express your emotions to anyone, or feel like you need to process them internally, try out these journaling prompts to get yourself thinking:

> **Journaling Prompts for Expressing and Managing Emotions**
>
> - When was the last time you felt a really strong emotion? Describe the experience in detail— How did it end up? What did you do? How did you act?
> - Do you feel comfortable talking about your emotions with the people around you? If not, how have you tried expressing yourself in the past? How effective has this been?
> - How intensely would you say you feel your emotions? (One being the lowest and ten being the most intense). Does this depend on the day or situation? Expand further.

LEARNING HOW TO SIT WITH YOUR EMOTIONS— STEPS TO FOLLOW

Sometimes it's hard to express your thoughts and feelings, and that is when you are going to need to step back, take a moment, and sit with what you are feeling. When you learn to recognize and listen to what your emotions are telling you, understanding yourself and what you are feeling will become so much easier! Here are a few steps to sitting with your emotions and processing them… not pushing them down.

1. Recognize that you are feeling a strong emotion. This might sound obvious, but this is a step a lot of us forget about when we are trying to process

our emotions. Simply admit that you are feeling *something*, regardless of if it's positive or negative. Then this step is where the five primary emotions list comes in handy!

2. Give a name to your feeling— Being able to properly communicate and identify *what* you are feeling is the next step.

3. Breathe— When you give a name to your emotions and are able to understand what you are feeling, calming exercises will help you get through processing these emotions. Sit down somewhere safe and comfortable, close your eyes, and inhale deeply. Counting your breaths, relaxing your body, and letting peace wash over you are great ways of practicing breathing to recenter yourself.

4. Keep a feelings journal— A journal dedicated to your emotions is a great way of allowing yourself to process them and sit with them. Your feelings journal can be filled with many different prompts. You can journal about specific emotions you feel throughout your day, what kinds of emotions you feel in a day, and simply express what you are going through. Sometimes just writing things out can help you recognize your emotions and understand what you are going through.

5. Learning reaction vs. response— A *reaction* is a quick and triggered response to something that happens to you. Reactions aren't usually thought out and are based completely on the emotions you are feeling at the moment. But a response takes time to process what is going on, helps you return to the situation, and can keep relationships from being hurt. Reactions often cause us to say things we don't mean, or do things based on intense emotions.

HOW BAD MENTAL HEALTH AFFECTS YOU

Mental health is just as important to your overall well-being as physical health. Bad mental health is a lot more intense than just feeling a little sad now and then. It can impact a lot of different areas of your life. If you experience poor mental health you might find yourself struggling in school, having a hard time making friends, struggling with decision-making, and not wanting to do things you normally enjoy.

Mental health can become a habit, and if you create bad mental health habits as a teen they will carry over into your adult life. Poor mental health is linked to other behavioral issues such as bullying and violence, drug or alcohol use, higher risk of dangerous sexual behaviors which can lead to STDs or even unwanted pregnancy.

So, what can you do to have better mental health habits and take better care of yourself?

THE BASICS OF GOOD MENTAL HEALTH

There are some great things you can do to help improve your mental health. Below are some tips you can remember when times get tough, and to prevent yourself from having poor mental health:

- Healthy body = healthy mind— Keeping your body active and eating the right foods actually has a massive impact on your mental health. Regular exercise greatly improves emotional health, relieves stress, helps you sleep better, and boosts the "happy" hormones in your brain!
- Relaxation practices— Practicing relaxation exercises on a regular basis to calm yourself down, show yourself some love, and reset after a long day are very helpful in improving overall mental health. Yoga, meditation, taking a long shower or bath, or practicing deep breathing can all help lower stress levels.
- Getting enough sleep— Sleep is key to our overall health, which includes our mental health as well. It really matters a lot more than you would think. When you have enough sleep you are able to think more clearly, emotionally regulate better, and reset your body in a healthy way.
- Prioritize fun— Letting yourself have fun on a regular basis will make you feel so much happier when it becomes a habit. We can all get really busy, but by scheduling time to have leisure, be with friends, and do things you enjoy, you can cultivate better mental health.

Questions and Prompts For Your Personal Diary

1. What are the most common emotions you find yourself experiencing out of the five primary emotions listed above?
2. Do you feel comfortable pausing and processing your emotions quietly? If so, what do you like doing most?
3. Would you say you are good at expressing your emotions in healthy ways? How do you usually express yourself to the people around you?
4. What is something you like to do for fun? Is it relaxing for you?
5. How are you going to use good mental health practices starting this week?

While your emotions are changing a lot during your teenage years, your body will be changing a lot as well. This can be stressful, and feel almost like you don't recognize yourself anymore. It is important to create a good sense of body image as a teen because that will carry over into your adult years. The next chapter is all about body image and positivity!

CHAPTER 5
BODY IMAGE

Society and the media surrounding us constantly give girls strict, unrealistic, and damaging goals for their bodies. The search for a "perfect body" or to look like the models on social media can be heavy… and it seriously affects self-confidence. The term "body image" just refers to how you view your body and how you feel about your physical appearance.

You are changing so much throughout your teenage years, and with low self-esteem piled on top of bad body image, the risk of depression and poor mental health increases. If you are struggling to accept the way you look, or have a hard time looking in the mirror, you are not alone. This is something so many people struggle with, but there are steps you can take to feel better and gain confidence in yourself!

WHAT IS BODY DYSMORPHIA?

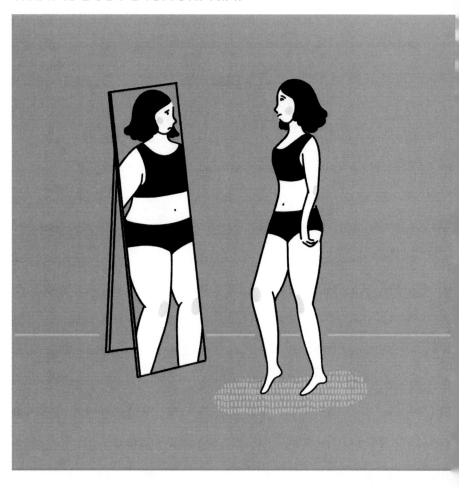

The first step in learning to love the body you were given is to understand the term "body dysmorphia." This simply means that a person tends to believe that their body or a part of their body looks ugly. A warped view of their body and seeing a different version of themselves in the mirror is the main problem faced by people with body dysmorphia.

People who struggle with this may think that they look good one day, then bad the next. It is a constant rollercoaster of emotions, and the person might not even be sure what they actually look like anymore.

These are some signs you might be struggling with body dysmorphia (Lyness, 2018):

- Focusing an extreme amount of attention on your looks. You might find yourself focusing on a specific thing you want to change about yourself, like the shape of your nose or legs.
- When you see yourself in the mirror or think about your looks it causes you to feel intense anxiety, anger, or worry.
- You are trying to fix your looks all the time, adjusting your clothes, fixing your hair, and going to the bathroom to check yourself in the mirror. The thoughts about your looks might take over your whole experience.
- You try not to be seen, have anxiety going out, and cover yourself with makeup and baggy clothes.

But body dysmorphia and poor body image don't need to be your reality. It's all a matter of changing your mindset and focusing your energy on different things.

WHAT ARE BODY POSITIVITY AND BODY NEUTRALITY?

The world around us pushes one ideal body type and makes the people who don't look like that feel like they are ugly. But the body positivity movement is all about learning to love your body and think of it in a positive way no matter how you look or how popular culture says you should look. Body positivity works to challenge the damaging perspective that social media is feeding us and make the world a more accepting place. It also promotes the acceptance of all bodies, as long as people love themselves and take care of their physical well-being. This movement has helped many people gain self-confidence and break down unrealistic beauty standards as well.

However, if feeling 100 percent confident and happy (and fully body-positive) feels like a daunting task, body neutrality is another version of this movement you can work towards. The basics of body neutrality are stopping the hate and rude words against your body. If you are wanting to strive for a neutral view of your body, you will need to learn to accept yourself for what you can do, not necessarily how you look.

Even if you don't like what you look like, having a neutral view of your body means accepting how you are, moving on, and taking care of yourself.

To sum it up: body positivity focuses on loving how you look no matter what, and body neutrality focuses less on your looks and more on how you feel.

TIPS TO IMPROVE BODY IMAGE

All of that sounds nice, but creating a better image of your body in your mind can be hard. That's what we'll be going over in this section... specific steps you can take to improve your body image on a daily basis!

- Identify the triggers of your negative body thoughts— When you start to think bad things about yourself and your body, try to make a mental note of what is happening. Where were you? Who were you with? Were you looking in the mirror? Were you wearing a certain outfit? All of these things can be triggers for negative body image moments.

- Combat those negative thoughts with positive affirmations— As soon as you catch yourself being rude to your body, it's time to use positive affirmations. Here is a list you can use to help combat negative body image and tell yourself the truth:

"I am beautiful inside and out."

"My body is the least interesting thing about me."

"I am proud of who I am, how I look, and how I dress."

"I love how smart I am."

"I look exactly how I am supposed to look."

- Clean out your social media— Social media and unrealistic beauty standards play a big role in making us think bad things about ourselves. You can start to carefully pick what you are seeing daily by going through the people you are following and *unfollowing* anyone who makes you feel bad about yourself. If you immediately hate yourself after seeing certain people online and begin comparing your body to theirs… hit the unfollow button.
- Focus on your strengths— Your body is a tool that has taken you through your whole life. It has changed, adapted, and grown, and how you look is not the main priority. It's time to start focusing on your physical and mental strengths and abilities. So, sit down with a pen and a piece of paper and try to write out at least five non-physical things about yourself that you admire. This might be your creativity, your ability to dance, your singing, your compassion, or your intelligence, for example.
- Stop comparisons— Again, comparison is the biggest killer of self-esteem. It can be hard to look at people and not compare yourself to them, but it is necessary. Everyone is unique, looks different, and has different strengths… and that is an awesome thing! So, when you start to focus on what makes you unique and see other girls as unique (and not competition) your self-confidence and body image will increase!
- Surround yourself with people who are also striving for body positivity— One of the best ways to become more body-positive is by

making friends with the right people. Maybe you follow body positivity accounts on social media, or maybe you need to make new friends. However you choose to do it… if you are surrounding yourself with people on the same journey, your path will be lined with encouragement!

Your body is beautifully unique, and learning to take care of it is a whole different story. The next chapter is all about how you can take care of your hair and skin to embrace your natural beauty!

CHAPTER 6
HAIR AND SKINCARE— IT MATTERS!

Learning to love your natural hair can be tricky. There are some ways you can style it, some products you can use, and practices you can do to embrace it! Whether it's straight, curly, thick, or thin, your hair and its care are important things for every budding woman to learn.

EMBRACING YOUR NATURAL HAIR

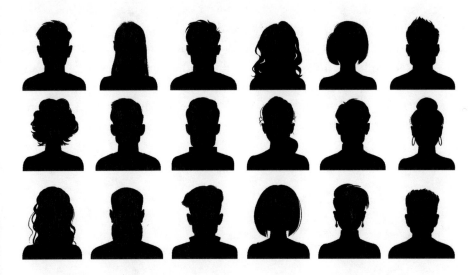

It's time to start thinking about how beautiful and unique your natural hair is. Even if you can't seem to tame it or it won't hold a curl, that's just how you were made! So, rather than trying your hardest to change the way your hair is, embracing it will do you so much better. Your hair is something that makes you unique. However, the pressure to blend in with your friends and classmates can be tough. Here are some more tips for learning to love your natural hair type:

Pinpoint what is bothering you— Maybe you want to straighten your curly hair because it gets frizzy... but there are actually things you can do to help with frizz! Sometimes it's as simple as finding the right *curly hair* or *thin hair* conditioner and shampoo. It probably isn't your whole head of hair that you are disagreeing with... so figuring out the problems is a great place to start embracing what you were born with!

Drop the heat tools— You might feel like you need to straighten or curl your hair to look "normal." But how are you ever going to learn to embrace your natural hair if you are always changing it? Styling tools actually damage your hair, dry it out, and make your hair break. If you feel like you aren't comfortable wearing your natural hair unstyled, you can try out some braids, a bun, or a ponytail.

Try out a new style— Sometimes, the problem is that we get bored with our hair, so trying out a new style is a great way of switching things up and learning to love your natural locks! You can experiment with different cuts and styles and find so many different ways to play with your beautiful hair. Curly hair can look really cool with a fun updo, and straight hair can easily play around with different braids. Short hair can be styled in so many fun half-up styles and with headbands and accessories! Seeing all the different things you can do with your natural hair can be an amazing way to embrace your natural beauty!

HAIR MAINTENANCE TIPS

Hair maintenance is another massive part of loving yourself and your natural hair, and taking care of your looks. Every head of hair is different, and there are so many care techniques, products, and routines that work for each individual. However, there are some basic hair maintenance tips that every girl should know when learning about taking care of her hair:

- Go for a trim every six to eight weeks to keep your ends fresh and healthy! If you don't get your hair styled or trimmed on a regular basis the ends can get damaged and start breaking off… which is no fun at all.
- Only wash your hair every few days. You should not be washing your hair every day or even every other day. Shampoos are great when they are made for your hair, but used too often they will strip your hair of healthy and natural oils that keep your locks strong.
- If you have naturally oily hair, you should wash it more often. This will mean something different to each person… but a general rule of thumb is to only wash when your hair actually *feels* dirty (or oily).
- Be sure to use a good helping of conditioner after every wash. Since shampoo takes the moisture out of your hair, you are going to need to rehydrate with a conditioner after each wash session.
- Skip the 2-in-1. These shampoos (and advertised conditioners) are not healthy for your hair and don't provide enough moisture.
- Be sure to choose a shampoo specifically for your hair type. Do you have dandruff? There will be a shampoo for you. Curly hair? Oily hair? No matter what your hair type, make sure you're using the *right* products.

Hair products can be hard to choose from… There are so many available. But don't let this scare you. If you are nervous to start picking out hair products, there are a few ingredients you should be looking to avoid. These ingredients damage hair or suck good moisture and include sulfates, silicones, synthetic fragrances, mineral oils, parabens, and denatured alcohols.

These might sound like a lot of big, confusing words… but a bottle should have it advertised on the front if it doesn't have these ingredients.

SKINCARE TIPS

Skincare is equally as important as haircare for teenage girls to learn about. It can be hard to know where to start, and simply going to the store to buy products gets you nowhere. So here are some skincare tips that every teen girl should know when starting her journey of taking care of her skin:

- Keep your routine simple. Overcomplicating your skin care routine can make it hard to stick to and even overwhelm your skin (and make you break out). A basic routine of gentle face wash and moisturizer twice each day is a great place to start.
- Never sleep with your makeup on! Even "skin-friendly" makeup can make you get more acne if you sleep with it on. If you are too tired to wash your face, you can even use a makeup remover wipe… just don't leave your makeup on your face. Wear sunscreen even if it's cloudy or wintertime. Sunscreen (meant for your face) protects your skin from harmful UV rays, prevents aging, and keeps your skin from getting irritated and causing more acne.

- Wash your sheets and pillows regularly. Your face will be touching your pillowcase and sheets every night and a lot of bacteria can build up there. Regularly changing your sheets can help prevent irritation and acne.
- Reach for "oil-free" and "non-comedogenic" products. If a product is labeled like this it means that it won't clog your pores and cause a breakout. This should be how you pick out face washes, sunscreens, moisturizers, and even makeup.
- Drink plenty of water! The magic drink that we all need is the biggest secret to healthy, glowing skin.
- Stop touching and picking at your face. It can be easy to rub your face or pick at a pimple, but doing this only irritates your skin more and can give you even more acne. This also means choosing gentle products that don't over-exfoliate, dry out or scrub your skin.
- Eating a balanced diet is another great way of balancing yourself from the inside out, giving yourself glowing and acne-free skin.

> **Questions and Prompts For Your Personal Diary— Creating a Hair and Skincare Plan!**
> 1. What are your biggest struggles with your hair?
> 2. What is one thing you can do to combat these struggles?
> 3. What are some of your favorite ways to style your hair? Make a list of your favorite styles and come back to it when you need inspiration!
> 4. What is your current skincare routine? How are you going to change it after reading this section?

So you know a lot about body image, confidence, and skin and hair care... but what about style? It can be hard to figure out what to wear, what you like, and what style to stick to. In the next chapter, we will talk all about how to experiment with your looks, find your style, and express yourself with your clothes!

CHAPTER 7
FINDING YOUR STYLE

Even if you feel like you need to dress a certain way because you always have, or because of how your friends dress… it's time to break free! There are so many different styles, fits, textures, colors, and patterns out there. Who knows what you might like? You are entering a new chapter as a teenager, and your parents are no longer the ones choosing your clothes and outfits, but that can be scary. This chapter will guide you through how to find your personal style, specific dressing tips, the power of accessories, different aesthetics, and how to dress best for your body!

STYLING TIPS

There are a lot of tips you can follow to get a better sense of style, and dress in a way that speaks to you. Below are some great ways to start experimenting and dressing how you actually want to.

Keep it simple— The biggest mistake people make when trying to figure out their personal style is that they overcomplicate everything. When you have a good closet full of the basics (white and black t-shirts, a good pair of jeans, a nice black dress, etc.) you can start to expand and style these clothes with anything. So, if you are just starting to revamp your wardrobe, start it off with good basics and neutral colors that can be styled in many different ways.

Stay away from trends— Trends are always coming and going, especially with social media today. This means that buying a piece one day may not be cool anymore in a few weeks. You will never be able to find your own personal style if you are always trying to keep up with trends.

Make sure it fits— To look your best you need to make sure you feel your best, and clothes that are too big or too small will not help you out. Fashion is all about making sure you are confident and comfortable. You should not be striving to fit into a certain size, because clothes are meant to fit *you*. When you wear the right clothes that fit your body in a comfortable way you will automatically feel more confident and comfortable in your own skin. Happiness and a beautiful smile are the true basis of style!

Style based on your personality— Fashion is a reflection of your personal interests and personality. This means that if you are a quieter person you might be more drawn to quieter clothes and simple beauty. But if you are loud and creative you may gravitate toward brighter colors, statement pieces, and experimentation. You should dress in a way that makes you happy, not how others want you to dress.

Keep to your values— Compromising your personal beliefs and values to fit in will never make you feel your best. If you aren't comfortable with low-cut tops, don't wear them. Being bold and fashionable doesn't always mean a short skirt and v-neck… whatever makes you feel confident is what you should stick to!

Accentuate your best features— It is no secret that some styles fit differently on different bodies. If you have long legs and want to highlight them, certain skirts or a good-fitting pair of jeans will help you out. Maybe you love to highlight your waist, so belts and high-waisted pants might be your go-to!

In the next section, we will go over the different body types, and styles that are usually the most flattering for each. Just remember that this is a simple guide and you can dress however you feel most confident.

FINDING YOUR BODY TYPE— STYLES THAT SUIT YOU

Each and every single body is uniquely beautiful, and it would be impossible to talk about every shape and size of body out there. However, there are a few body types that most women and girls fit into, regardless of size. This is simply about the way your body is structured, with some tips on what is most flattering on each body type! The goal of dressing for your body type isn't to try and make yourself look different or like you have a different body type, it's all about finding what makes you look confident!

Pear shape:

You may have a pear-shaped body if:

- Your waist or hips are bigger than your shoulders (or bust).
- Your hips, rear, and thighs are fuller.
- Your shoulders are considered narrow.

Some of the best styles that flatter pear-shaped bodies include:

- A-line dresses and skirts that flow out past (or above) the waist.

- Flowy tops. Play around with them! More volume on your bust and shoulders will balance your body out beautifully.
- Big earrings and layered necklaces look amazing on you!
- Plunging v-necks, scoop necks, and boxy shapes will flatter your chest nicely!

Hourglass shape:

You may have an hourglass-shaped body if:

- Your body is considered "curvy."
- Your waist is well-defined and smaller than your bust and hips.
- You have a fuller bust, hips, and thighs.
- You have broader shoulders that are about equal measurements with your hips.

Some of the best styles that flatter hourglass-shaped bodies include:

- Wrap tops that accentuate your waist.
- Anything with a v-neck, round neck, or boxy neckline.
- Dresses that tie or hit at the waist will look awesome on you! If you love a flowy dress, simply adding a belt can look great too!
- High-waisted skirts.
- Hip-hugging pants.

Apple or inverted triangle shape:

You may have an apple-shaped body if:

- Your shoulders are equal or broader than your hips.
- Your hips and thighs aren't necessarily full or curvy.
- You don't have a super-defined waist.

Some of the best styles that flatter apple-shaped bodies include:

- A-line anything!
- Flowy tunics and dresses will look lovely on you.
- V-neck anything.

- Wrap dresses and maxi styles are stunning!
- Oversized tunics or sweaters paired with leggings or skinny jeans.

Rectangle or athletic shape:

You may have an athletic-shaped body if:

- You aren't considered curvy.
- Your shoulder, waist, and hip measurements are close to the same.
- Your waist isn't super well-defined.
- Your weight is fairly evenly distributed across your body

Some of the best styles that flatter athletic-shaped bodies include:

- Racer back styles in tops and dresses.
- Halter necklines.
- Strapless anything.
- Open back and halter dresses.
- Flowly dresses with belts will look amazing on you!

A GUIDE TO ACCESSORIES

The best way to dress up those basic outfits I just mentioned is by adding accessories. Even if you only have neutral-colored clothes you can make anything into a bold outfit with the right statement pieces and accessories. Below are some must-have accessories and how to use them to improve your style and fashion.

A chic handbag— Every girl needs a go-to handbag that can be used on many different occasions. A nice black bag (that fits all of your items) and that you can add on top of any style or outfit is a must for any girl!

Classic sunglasses that flatter your face— Sunglasses are another great accessory that can add personality and class to your outfits. Investing in a decent pair will help you look more put together and well-dressed. You just need to let yourself experiment with shapes and colors to find a pair that suits you best!

Know your best metals— Gold, rose gold, and silver look different on different skintones. When you discover what metals look best on you, start to only buy jewelry in those colors. This way all of your pieces match and make you look more put together. The right jewelry will add a bit of glamour to your outfits without being too crazy.

Statement pieces — Choosing a single statement piece (maybe bold earrings, a long necklace, or colorful bag) is a great way to bring personality and color to your outfits. A beautiful jacket can make any plain black outfit and sneakers look put together. It's all a matter of choosing what you like to add on top of your basics.

Lastly, a good rule to keep when adding pieces to your outfits is that understated accessories pair well with bold outfits and neutral outfits pair best with bold accessories.

DIFFERENT AESTHETICS TO TRY OUT

There are so many different styles out there, how do you even pick one to try out? Here's a list you can look over to help solve this problem.

See what speaks to you! Try out the different aesthetics that feel most like your personality and watch as your fashion sense grows and develops! Each of the styles below are just classic personality and fashion styles. There are many more out there, so these are just a few of the basics.

Traditional

The traditional aesthetic is classy and refined. The traditional-dressing woman shops minimally and looks to buy basic pieces she can wear for years to come. Her clothes never go out of style and are always clean-cut. Most of the time women who dress traditionally stick to business casual outfits with blazers, nice skirts, clean button-downs, and sleek feminine dresses.

Elegant

The elegant style is similar to traditional but is a bit less formal. In this aesthetic, a woman will stick to solid and neutral colors, rarely choosing anything patterned. But her beauty lies in her natural looks, clean makeup, and accessories. She makes sure to be discreet, but beautifully feminine.

Natural Casual

The natural casual style is simple, not very formal, and incorporates a lot of natural colors and fabrics. This may be a good style for you to try out if you prefer cotton, neutral and warm colors, minimalism, few accessories, and little to no makeup. The women who dress like this are often very confident in themselves and only wear items they know will be comfortable.

Sporty Casual

This style is one of the most common styles out there for teenagers. It is simple, comfortable, and fun. Women who dress sporty casual will be seen in jeans, t-shirts, leggings, and sneakers most of the time. These women often play around with different textures, colors, and prints, showing off bright and fun colors to match their bright, fun, and casual personalities.

Romantic

The romantic aesthetic is definitely the most classically feminine style. You can feel feminine wearing any clothes, but if you are more "girly" and pride yourself on your feminine side, this might be a good style to experiment with. The romantic style incorporates light and delicate colors, flowy silhouettes, dresses and skirts, ruffles, high-heels, ballet flats, floral prints, and lots of pink!

Creative

Creative women always seem to be in a happy mood. They express their uniqueness through bold colors, textures, prints, and styles. This aesthetic just needs to reflect your imagination, combining the different elements you enjoy. The creative woman's wardrobe is full of fun bags, cute prints and fabrics, and lots of accessories.

Dramatic

The dramatic style is very modern, fashionable, put together, and bold. The woman who dresses in the dramatic style often wears statement accessories, abstract prints, bright colors, and unique pieces. These women are constantly exploring different aspects of fashion and their style may change on a daily basis.

Questions and Prompts For Your Personal Diary— Planning Your Wardrobe!

1. How would you describe yourself and your personality?
2. Does your current style reflect who you are?
3. What is your favorite style you see on other girls?
4. Now, plan out 3 different outfits you want to wear this week to experiment with your style!

Now it's time to talk about physical health, hygiene, and feminine health practices. The tips in the next chapter are essential for any budding young woman to learn!

CHAPTER 8
MAINTAINING YOUR PHYSICAL HEALTH AND HYGIENE

There are a lot of different things that help make you physically healthy. Your mind and body are deeply connected, and when you discover a good balance of healthy eating, moving your body, listening to what your body needs, and getting enough sleep you will feel so good! This chapter is all about how to create a balanced lifestyle, how to take care of yourself as a girl, and the dangers of eating disorders.

A BALANCED LIFESTYLE

Keeping yourself healthy is all about learning balance and moderation. You don't need to go to the gym every day or eat salads every meal in order to be healthy and happy. Taking care of your body starts with listening to what it needs. Hungry? Eat. Thirsty? Drink. Your body will give you the signals to what it requires. Below are more tips for living a healthier lifestyle:

The 80/20 rule— The 80/20 rule is a good way to measure balance in your diet and eating patterns. Health is all about moderation, so trying to eat healthy and whole food 80% of the time, eating fun food, sugar, and even fast foods the other 20% offers great freedom. Eating junk isn't the best thing for you, and you might not feel great after but letting yourself have *all* the foods you enjoy is a great way to bring balance to your life. This might look like eating healthy meals, then having a dessert. Or maybe eating mostly well during the week and then having pizza for dinner one night. Moderation is key here!

Getting enough sleep— Sleep is a critical piece of our overall health. Getting enough sleep (the recommended eight to ten hours for teens) is beneficial for your physical and mental development. If you are sleeping enough you can actually reduce levels of anxiety, build up your brain, and help your muscle growth after exercise. In order to get a good night's sleep try to put away electronics at least thirty minutes before bedtime, limit caffeine and foods high in sugar in the hours leading up to sleep, and create a soothing environment by blocking lights and shutting out noises.

Moving your body in an enjoyable way— Exercise is undoubtedly good for you, but punishing yourself in the gym and pushing yourself too hard is not. This can damage your emotional well-being and make you associate negative feelings with movement. However, moving your body is highly important for emotional, mental, and physical health. This just means that setting realistic goals and moving in ways you enjoy will be key. You can do this by taking a walk around your neighborhood, joining a team sport, or even dancing around your living room.

Learning to manage stress— Stress levels and anxiety can be high during your teenage years, with learning to navigate school, life, and friends, but stress can do crazy things to your body. It can make you exhausted and unable to focus, and even give you acne and make you bloated. This means that if you are able to manage stress and soothe yourself, your life will be much healthier and more balanced! Try to discover stress management techniques that work for you. Examples you can experiment with are exercising, doing some yoga, journaling, listening to music, dancing, reading, or just sitting by yourself in peace and quiet.

FEMININE HYGIENE QUICK TIPS

Feminine hygiene is a very important aspect of overall health as a woman. By learning to take care of your feminine parts you will protect yourself from infections, which is an essential part of female health. Below are some quick tips you can follow to make sure you are taking proper care of yourself:

- Bathe regularly— Taking showers and baths at the end of the day or after a workout is just as important as specifically cleaning your female parts. Simply showering off regularly is essential to your feminine health.
- Proper cleaning— Even if you are bathing regularly, you also need to be sure you are cleaning your private parts properly. This means rinsing with water and gentle soap. Your female parts are sensitive and you should avoid any products that have chemicals or harsh ingredients in them, including fragrances.
- Only ever wash the outside of your vagina— The inside actually has a method of self-cleaning. This means that you don't need to be worried about cleaning, scrubbing, or rinsing the *inside* of your vagina at all. Soaps of pretty much any kind will irritate you and throw off the whole operation.
- No fragrances— Products, including soaps, with fragrances contain irritating chemicals that will not be helpful when cleaning and caring for your private parts. In fact, some chemicals in scented soaps can cause serious infections.
- Hygiene during menstruation— The most important time to take careful care of yourself is during your period. Everyone wants to feel

clean and comfortable at that time of the month, so to make this easier make sure you are regularly switching out pads and tampons as well as washing with water more often.
- Cotton underwear is the best— Cotton is a very breathable fabric and underwear made of it is best for everyday wear. It allows your vagina to breathe and gives space for excess moisture and discharge to evaporate.

A GUIDE TO PERIODS

Now it's time to go over some of the most commonly asked questions in regard to periods and the female menstrual cycle. Knowing how to take care of yourself also includes understanding your period. Your period happens when blood is released from your uterus and comes out through the vagina. When you get your first period it is one of the biggest signs that you are nearing the end of puberty.

How long should periods last?	The average period will last around 5 days, but it is normal to experience shorter periods (around 3 days) when you first get yours. And even periods lasting up to 8 days are totally normal.
How often do periods come?	In the beginning, they will likely be irregular. But as time goes by, you should expect your period to come every 4 to 5 weeks.
When is it normal to get my period?	On average, girls tend to get their period around 12 years old. However, it is totally normal to get your first period any time between 10 and 15.
What products should I use?	Pads, tampons, and menstrual cups… which to use?! • Pads are sticky strips of cotton that stick to your underwear. Most girls start off with pads when they first get their period. • Tampons are more convenient to use than pads when swimming or playing sports. A tampon is inserted into the vagina and catches blood before it exits. Tampons should not be left in for more than eight hours. • Menstrual cups are a reusable alternative, however, they can be daunting for younger users. They are cups made of silicon that are inserted into the vagina and need to be emptied at least every twelve hours.
What is PMS?	PMS (also known as premenstrual syndrome) happens when you experience both physical and emotional symptoms and mood swings before and during your period. Some symptoms include sadness, acne, anxiety, bloating, and moodiness.
Can I stop cramps?	You may experience cramping in your lower stomach before or during your period. In order to help ease them try taking ibuprofen, using a heating pack, or taking a hot bath.
How do I know if my period is normal?	Here are a few signs to look for and see if your period isn't normal: • You haven't gotten your period by age 15 • You have an irregular period (after having it for 2 years) • You have to change your pad or tampon more than once every two hours. • You bleed between periods.

If you experience any of the signs of an abnormal period, don't worry because they are often very common and won't be an issue. However, you should still head over to a doctor to get it checked or talk to a parent just in case.

Periods are totally normal, and they are nothing to feel embarrassed about. Every girl will have one and even if they feel taboo to talk about, they are something completely natural. Accidents will happen. The thing is that every girl with a period has experienced it! You might bleed through your pad or tampon and onto your pants, and it won't be fun. Again, this is nothing to be embarrassed about. Here are a few tips on how you can prevent accidents from happening, and on how you can cover them up:

- Change your products regularly— One of the best ways to prevent leaks is by making sure you are switching out your pad or tampon *before* it gets too full. Over time you will figure out what days your period is heaviest and change your period products as needed.
- Be prepared— You may start your period while you are out in public, you might need to change your pad or tampon out of the house, and you might have a friend who needs some help. As a girl, it is always best to be prepared and keep a "period kit" with a change of underwear, a few extra pads, and a few extra tampons on hand. You can keep this in your purse, car, or school backpack.
- Carry a sweater with you— If you have experienced period leaks in the past and aren't quite sure you can prevent them, just take the above precautions and carry around a sweater with you in public! This might not be the most practical, but if you do leak through your pants you will have something to cover up with.

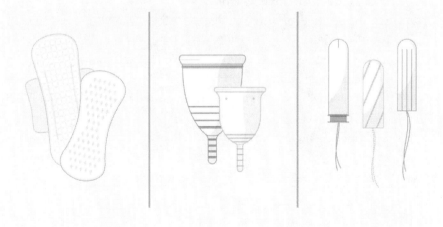

EATING ENOUGH

Eating disorders are very common in young girls, but this does not mean they are healthy or okay. Part of taking care of your body is listening to what it needs, not restricting yourself to only "healthy" foods, and not overindulging. There are different kinds of eating disorders, and they each manifest in different ways. An individual who is struggling with an eating disorder may also view it differently, even if the diagnosis is the same. Regardless of how it looks, unhealthy eating patterns are always dangerous.

There are four main categories of eating disorders, but even if someone was not diagnosed with an eating disorder they can still have disordered eating patterns. Unhealthy eating patterns and a bad view of food are just as dangerous as an eating disorder.

An eating disorder (or generally unhealthy eating pattern) can manifest as purposefully skipping meals, extreme fasting, constantly dieting, taking laxatives, and vomiting. These may be signs of an eating disorder or might be the beginning of one. If you struggle with any thoughts of starving yourself, throwing up, secretly eating, or other signs listed previously, please reach out to a trusted adult. They will be able to get you the help you need and guide you to a happier and healthier life.

Other forms of disordered eating include:

- Constantly fluctuating weight.
- Feeling guilty every time you eat, whether what you're eating is healthy or not.
- Always thinking about weight, appearance, and food… to the point where it negatively impacts your life.
- Using exercising as a way to reduce calories after you eat "bad" foods.
- Feeling like you can't control yourself around food and always over eating.

The four main eating disorders include the following:

Anorexia Nervosa— This eating disorder manifests as not eating much, or not eating at all. This includes both solid and liquid foods. These unhealthy eating patterns often come from a belief that any amount of food (or certain type of food) will cause weight gain. Someone who struggles with anorexia nervosa will likely perceive themselves as "fat" or overweight, even if they are severely underweight. This eating disorder may also include exercising too much and even purging through laxatives and vomiting.

Binge-Eating Disorder— Binge eating refers to excessively eating a ton of food in a very short period of time, most times hidden away from other people. This period of eating will be uncontrollable and will go until the person is uncomfortably full. Binge eating is most often triggered by something that makes the person look for comfort in food. After an episode of binge eating people often feel guilt, shame, and self-hatred.

Bulimia Nervosa— Bulimia Nervosa is linked directly to binge-eating disorder. The difference here is that when the feeling of guilt comes after a binge eating episode, bulimics purge by self-induced vomiting, over exercising, extreme fasting, or use of laxatives.

Orthorexia Nervosa— This is a lesser known eating disorder, but the problem is that it often goes unnoticed and undiagnosed. Orthorexia nervosa refers to an obsession with exercise and eating healthy. The people struggling with this eating disorder will refuse to eat a list of specific foods that they consider unhealthy, otherwise known as "fear foods." This eating disorder, if left unnoticed, can even turn into anorexia and full starvation attempts (*Eating disorders* 2022).

If you believe that you are struggling with an eating disorder, thoughts of disordered eating and food guilt, or unhealthy eating patterns, I encourage you to seek help. Your body needs food… food is fuel. To simply exist, your body needs it to survive. But it also should not be used as a form of comfort. Again, life is all about finding balance.

Here are a few tips for reaching out to a parent or trusted adult about your struggles:

- One way to go about this is to try to bring it up casually. Don't make a huge deal about it and worry them. This way you are both relaxed and can open a conversation where you can talk about your struggles.
- You can also try to set a time and a place with a trusted adult and let them know that you need to talk to them. This can help you work up the courage and get ready for a specific moment you have set.
- Use the right terminology. If you aren't sure if you are struggling with a specific eating disorder let them know you are experiencing "disordered eating patterns." If you have pinpointed what you may be experiencing, use the right name. This helps them know you are serious about what you are talking about and will help them understand you better.

Reaching out for help and advice can be daunting, but it is the first step in becoming your happiest and healthiest self.

> **Questions and Prompts For Your Personal Diary**
>
> 1. As you are getting older have you noticed changes in your diet or body? If so, what? (Maybe you started packing your own lunch or not eating as much.)
> 2. What sorts of exercise do you enjoy? Are you going to try and incorporate this into your daily routine?
> 3. What is your relationship with food like? Do you tend to not care, or is it a point of stress for you?
> 4. Have you ever thought you had an eating disorder?
> 5. Did the explanations above of eating disorders (and disordered eating) describe you?

Learning to take care of your physical body starts with daily care, but you are also going to need to know what to do in an emergency. In the next chapter we will be talking all about basic first aid skills, what to do in a crisis, and tips that every adult and *teen* needs to know in order to keep themselves safe.

CHAPTER 9
FIRST AID SKILLS

Another essential life skill is knowing how to respond to physical ailments in an emergency, also known as first aid. These skills aren't just about putting a bandage on a wound, they are about bug stings, ankle sprains, and any other injury that may come up.

RULES TO REMEMBER BEFORE GIVING FIRST AID

Creating a first aid kit is a very good start to learning about safety. However, there are some basic rules about first aid that you need to know before you create your kit. Here are the rules you will need to remember before offering first aid:

- Assess the situation before acting. You need to take note of what is going on and what supplies you have before ever starting to physically help someone.
- If an infection is present, protect yourself before you help.
- Check and see if you can help alone or if you need help from an adult or someone else.
- Offer comfort and soothing words to whoever is injured.

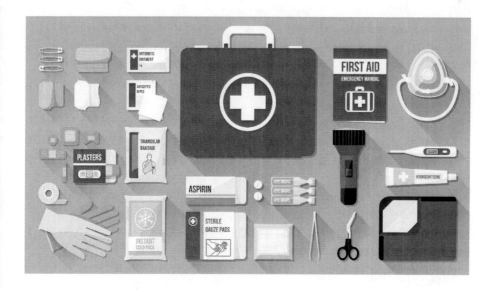

So now you're ready to actually make your own first aid kit. Here are the steps to do so:

CREATING AND KEEPING A FIRST AID KIT

Step 1: Decide the size and container of the kit. You need to consider what items you might include and where the kit is going to be. It needs to fit nicely in a specific space and not get in the way (or you might move it and lose it). For example, if it is going in your school backpack it should only be a small bag of essentials. But if it is a family first aid kit it might be bigger (like the size of a lunch tin). You will also need to make sure that the container can be sealed or locked.

Step 2: Add emergency numbers. It is important to include a list of the emergency numbers for your local area in your first aid kit, should you ever need them.

Step 3: It's time to pack your items. Below is a checklist of the basic items every first aid kit should include:

- A variety of bandages. Different sizes, shapes, and materials will be important.
- Antiseptic wipes

- Scissors
- Tweezers
- Antibiotic ointment
- Elastic bandage (like an ACE wrap)
- Disposable gloves
- Gauze pads
- Antiseptic solution (such as hydrogen peroxide)
- Adhesive tape
- Safety pins- to tie ends of bandages.

DIFFERENT AILMENTS AND HOW TO TREAT THEM IN AN EMERGENCY

Here we will cover the basics of different ailments, injuries, sicknesses, and emergencies you might encounter (The Nemours Foundation, 2023).

Ankle sprains

Signs and symptoms:

- Soreness and swelling around the ankle.
- Throbbing pain even without touching it.
- Having a hard time putting weight on your foot.
- Bruising in the injured area.

Treatments:

First, protect the ankle with a wrap to keep it from moving too much. Then be sure to rest the ankle, elevated above your heart, to reduce swelling and prevent more injury. You can then take some pain medicine, apply ice, and keep it compressed.

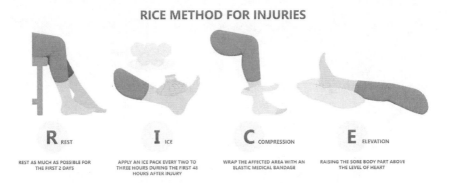

How to treat a burn

Burns can range from serious to mild. If your skin is extremely damaged or doesn't heal quickly, contact a doctor immediately.

Treatments:

First, cool the burn with cool, not overly cold, water. Next, remove clothing and jewelry around the area. From here, apply lotion or healing cream to calm down the burn. Then you can take a mild pain reliever while you keep the area bandaged to prevent further damage.

After it starts to heal, don't remove the blisters that may form.

Concussions

Signs and symptoms:

- Headache
- Blurry vision
- Nausea or vomiting
- Forgetting what happened
- Unclear speaking
- Confusion
- Taking a long time to answer simple questions

Treatments (only for *mild* concussions— if symptoms persist longer than a few hours, contact a doctor immediately):

- First, the person needs to relax at home or in a comfortable environment. However, do not let them fall asleep until the symptoms have gone away.
- Avoid screen time or at least minimize it.
- Don't let the concussed person drive.
- Avoid rough, exerting, or sports activities until symptoms go away.
- Take a light pain reliever for the headache.

Cuts and scratches

When someone first gets cut, try to immediately stop the bleeding. This can be done by holding a clean cloth or bandage against the wound until the bleeding stops. Do not lift up the bandage or cloth until you know the person has stopped bleeding, otherwise, it may start again.

From here, clean the wound with water and gentle soap. Then take an antibiotic ointment and cover the wound with a thin layer to kill any germs. Lastly, cover it with a bandage and avoid touching it.

Dehydration

Signs and symptoms:

- Feeling light-headed and dizzy

- Dry or sticky mouth
- Extreme fatigue
- Heated cheeks and face

Treatments:

Know the early signs of dehydration (being thirsty and having a headache) in order to prevent it from becoming too extreme. However, if someone is very dehydrated, offer them lots of liquids to help restore their body back to normal. If they are overheating, a cold shower (or a cold, wet towel) will be helpful. Drinks with electrolytes can also be very helpful.

Nose bleeds

Steps to stop them:

- Grab tissues to catch the blood.
- Stand or sit in an upright position.
- Tilt your head forward (not back)
- Pinch your nose together just below the bony part of your nose to help stop blood flow. It will typically stop within ten minutes.

WHEN DO I CALL FIRST RESPONDERS?

You should only call emergency responders when someone is in need of help immediately because of an injury or they are in danger. If you can help someone, or an adult around you can, and they will recover, then there is no need to call.

Here are a few examples of when it would be appropriate to call first responders:

- A fire
- Someone is unconscious after an accident
- Someone is having a hard time breathing or having an asthma attack
- Someone overdosed on drugs
- You see or experience a serious car accident
- Someone is choking and can't breathe
- If you or someone else is bleeding and you are unable to stop it
- You witness a crime happening (i.e: theft, mugging, break-ins, or violence).
- If you are distressed and are worried for the physical or mental health of yourself or an individual who poses a threat to others or themselves.

If you are curious to learn more, we will talk even more about safety skills, how to calm yourself down in overwhelming times, and dive deeper into how to react to emergencies and threats in *Chapter 12: Safety Skills and Self-Defense.*

CHAPTER 10
SMART MONEY

You might have just gotten your first job, or started saving more from your monthly allowance. However you got money, it's time to learn what to do with it. Sure, it's fun to save up and spend on yourself, but that's not how the real world works. You need to learn how to save your money, choose what to spend it on, and how to track what you are making and spending. When you become an adult you need to know how to manage your money, because expenses add up *really* fast.

Loans are another big part of life that school doesn't teach you about. In this chapter, we'll be going over different kinds of loans, how to get them, and everything you need to know before you get one.

BUDGETING 101

Learning to budget all starts with knowing and tracking your income. Being responsible with money means spending less than you make, in order to stay out of debt (or owing someone else money). To start, take one month to track everything you make. When you know how much is coming in each month, you then know your budget. From here it's just a matter of figuring out what to spend money on and how much. Below are great budgeting tips to get you started on managing your money:

Budgeting categories

One of the best ways to start budgeting and keeping to the amount of money you are making each month is to list out categories of expenses. You can start out with two categories: savings and spending. You can then list out what you will be spending your money on under each category. Some of the most common expenses you might list include *necessary spending* and *additional spending*. Here are some basic examples:

Necessary spending:

- Lunch money
- Gas for your car
- Phone bill
- Car payment

Additional spending:

- Subscriptions such as streaming or music services.
- Additional food or treats (coffee, ice cream, fast food, etc.)
- Clothes and shopping
- Additional activities (such as sports, hobbies, and extracurriculars, and outings with friends)
- Beauty tools and makeup

Most teens are not contributing to paying rent or other housing expenses, but if you do, feel free to add those expenses under *necessary* (Mint, 2022).

Additional budgeting strategies

50/ 30/ 20 rule— This daily budgeting system is simple and is based on spending your money in the following manner: 50 percent on necessities, 30 percent on additional spending, and 20 percent on savings. These percentages don't need to be non-negotiable but can be a great guideline to get started. You might want to put more toward savings, or less toward rent or other necessities.

"Going to zero" budgeting— This is a good budgeting style if you are looking to account for every dollar you make. If you use this method you are going

to need to know *exactly* what you make before starting. From there you will separate what you know you spend monthly, and divvy up the last amounts until you reach zero. This is your budget, and if you add money into savings you will benefit even more.

"Paying yourself first" — The name of this one might sound the best, but it doesn't mean treating yourself and spending your whole paycheck in one day. Instead "paying yourself first" means taking out a certain amount of money from your paycheck at the beginning of the month and putting it into savings. From there you have the rest of your money to spend on anything else you need or want to.

Needs vs. wants and smart shopping

Making money and spending it is easy, but spending your money in a smart way is a whole lot harder. Creating a list of your needs and your wants will be a great way to get started on becoming a smart shopper. When you are out with friends, or at the store looking to replace a clothing item, this list will help you stick to your budget.

When you pick something up and want it, ask yourself, "Do I actually need this?" This way you can take a moment to determine if you are spending your money in a wise way. Writing down all of the things you need to purchase in a month (or in the upcoming months) can be an awesome way of prioritizing what you spend.

Being careful with credit cards

You won't be able to open a credit card on your own until you turn 18. But if your parents get you one, this is a time to learn how to use one, and not spend recklessly. The problem with credit cards is that it can feel like "free money" since it isn't coming out of your bank account as you spend it. Credit card companies often have a "minimum payment" that you can make each month. However, if you spend more than what you pay as a minimum payment you are putting yourself in debt. This debt then has *massive* interest rates, basically meaning the longer it takes for you to pay it off, the more you have to pay.

To be smart with your credit cards be sure you know when you need to pay them off. And when the end of the month comes, be sure to pay off the whole thing. This means you are only spending money you have, you are not going into debt, and will be able to get other credit cards in the future because you have a good record.

Setting goals and tracking habits

Another great way to ensure you are sticking to a good budget is to set goals! Maybe you want to be able to buy a car, or are saving up for college. Whatever it is, these goals will keep you going. Keeping your spending low will be much easier when you have something to work towards.

When you have a goal and want to save a certain amount monthly, it's important to continuously track your spending habits. You can do this in a few different ways. However, the simplest way is to create a journal or physical place where you write down what you spent money on, how much, and when.

TIPS TO SAVE MORE

It can be a hard task to save for your first big purchase, or just work to grow a savings account. The easiest way to achieve these goals is to learn to make saving a habit. All you need is a plan and some patience… It won't happen overnight. Here are some simple tips to get used to saving:

- Figure out a number to add on a monthly basis and add it without fail— Once you know just how much you are making and how much you are spending, it's time to set aside money each month. This number will depend on your job and spending habits. But if you have a goal and are saving for something specific, being more disciplined with your goals will be much more doable.
- Make some spending switches— As we have talked about, tracking your spending is a great way to understand yourself and your habits. After a month or so of keeping a diary of everything you make and spend you will have a better idea of what you are spending *too much* on. Are you willing to go out for coffee once each week (and make it at home the other times) rather than three times every week? The small things add up, so even pinpointing one thing you can cut back on is extra money you can save.

Here is a quick example:

Let's say you go eat fast food or buy a sandwich three times every week because you are hungry after school and your bill is around ten dollars per meal. If you simply packed a meal from home, you could be saving 780 dollars in six months. It might not seem like a lot at the moment, but it all adds up.

- Have someone to encourage you— A parent or friend is a great person to have as an accountability partner. If someone else understands your savings goals, and you ask them for help, you can have someone reminding you on a regular basis of why you are trying to save money.
- Start using cash more often— This is just a great general budgeting tip: If you put a certain amount of money in savings *first* then take the rest out in cash… that's all you have. Spending with a credit or debit card is a great way to spend *more* money. When you are using cash you actually see the money leaving your hand and it makes you want to spend less.
- Create a vision board to remind yourself of your goals— Being constantly reminded of what you are saving for is one of the best ways to hold yourself accountable. It can be hard to keep yourself

focused if you have no end goal in mind. Keeping yourself accountable and remembering your "why" is a great way of staying on track.

Loans

A financial loan is money that is borrowed from either a person or a business for a specific purpose(*Loans 101 for Teens* 2023). When you take a loan you are making a promise to pay back the full amount as well as interest (extra money) depending on how long you take to pay it back. Loans can cover things like cars, business goals, college, and homes.

Important vocabulary— loans

- Interest: Additional money paid to a lender in exchange for the loan
- Interest rate: The percentage of the loan paid by the borrower as interest.
- Collateral: Something that holds value and that is given to the lender in case the borrower doesn't pay back the loan.
- Equity: How much a house is worth, subtracting the amount that is still owed to a lender.

(*Loans 101 for Teens* 2023)

Here are a few different types of loans and their purposes (*Loans 101 for Teens* 2023):

Personal loans— A personal loan can be used to do pretty much anything you want with it. The most common uses people take personal loans out for are medical emergencies, vacations, and even home furnishings and appliances. With personal loans, you will typically have to agree to a specific interest rate.

Car loans— These loans are used to purchase cars. The interest rates on auto loans are typically very low as the car will be used as collateral and will be taken away if you don't pay.

Student loans— These kinds of loans are going to be the most common type that you will use in the near future. They are used to pay for college tuition or other expenses of higher education. You can either apply for student loans from government programs or private companies and lenders. It is likely more interesting to go the route of federal programs because they have options to forgive the debt and even pay them off based on your income. However, private lenders usually don't offer these options.

Credit-building loans— If you weren't good at paying back your credit cards or just have a generally bad credit score, you can take out small loans to pay back in order to build your score. These are typically very small amounts of money with high interest that are paid back in a short period of time.

Mortgage loans— This kind of loan might not be immediately important to understand, but school doesn't teach it, so you need to learn about it somewhere! This kind of loan allows you to borrow money in order to buy a house, with the house as collateral. Usually, this kind of loan has quite low-interest rates.

TIPS FOR MANAGING LOANS

Not paying back loans means your debt adds up and you have to pay a lot more money in the future. Here are a few tips for managing loans if you need to take one out:

- Stick to a budget. You already learned how to do this, and if you are able to stick to those budgeting skills when you become an adult, a loan will be a lot easier to handle.
- Keep an emergency fund in your savings that is able to cover at least one month's worth of living expenses (including your loan payments).
- Avoid impulse buys as they might affect your ability to cover your loans later in the month.
- Create a good relationship with the person you are borrowing money from. This means that if your payment is going to be late one month they may be more understanding.

We talked a little bit about car loans, but there is so much more you need to know about buying your first car, its maintenance, and the responsibilities that come with its purchase. The next chapter will cover everything you need to know when buying your first car.

CHAPTER 11
A GUIDE TO YOUR FIRST CAR

Your first car is your first real taste of freedom as a teenager. There are so many things you need to take into account before buying your first car. Then, after you get a loan, find a car, and start making payments, how do you keep it running? This chapter will go over how to buy your first car as well as basic automotive skills everyone should know!

QUICK TIPS FOR BUYING YOUR FIRST CAR

- Set clear expectations before starting the search— Sit down with your parents or guardians and ask questions, set expectations, and get clear *together* exactly what you're looking for and what you can afford to pay. They may be willing to help you out financially, and they might have some expectations that they would like you to understand as well. Creating an open environment for conversations can be a great way to ask for advice and get started on this process.
- Shop for safety— Beyond just looking for a good price tag or a pretty car, shopping for safety is critical… Especially when purchasing your first car. Here are a few items on a car safety checklist that you should keep in mind when you go car shopping:

Make the most of your test drive— check the car for dents and any damage, check the tires for use, test the brake lights and turn signals, and make sure you test the car in stop-and-go traffic.

Drive on the highway where you need to get over 55 miles per hour.

Test how easy and safe it is to parallel park.

Ask the seller about any safety measures included.

- Consider whether new or used is better for you— Deciding if you want a new or used car is more than just a price difference. There are some pros and cons to each. If you are buying new, that higher price tag (and higher insurance) also comes with possible customization, better interest rates on a loan, and the fact that the vehicle is more reliable.

A used car can be significantly cheaper for monthly payments, will have lower insurance rates, and will lose value a lot slower than a new car. Obviously, this is the more cost-effective option, but there are some downsides to consider:

Used cars are more likely to have higher maintenance costs. These cars have already been worn in and it is important to take that into account. So, while the initial cost will likely be quite low, more repairs will be needed.

You don't know how the previous owners— If you are buying used from a stranger a risk you have to take is not knowing how they treated or fixed the car.

There is likely to be little to no warranty left— When you buy a used car you are buying it with whatever work needs to be done. So, if something needs to be fixed and there is no warranty, it will all fall to you.

Having to deal with problems earlier— Since the car has already been worn in, you may have to deal with issues sooner than if you purchased new.

LOANS AND THE PURCHASING PROCESS

While car loans for teens are a thing, they will be a bit harder to get than if you had a longer credit history. This is because auto lenders and auto financing companies prefer to give money to people who have proven to be responsible with loans in the past. Below are some tips to get your first car loan as well as other purchasing options available to you:

- Figuring out what loan path to take— If you haven't turned 18 yet it will be hard for you to be able to take out a car loan entirely on your own. This means a parent or other trusted adult can co-sign with you. If you have a family member signing with you this will likely increase your chances of getting a better loan. Since you likely have little to no credit, you can also look for a lender that specializes in loans for people without much credit.
- When you get the loan— It's time to start budgeting and making monthly payments. If you don't pay back on time you may lose your car or be charged higher fees.
- Consider other purchasing options— If you want to get a car but can't qualify for a loan or get someone to co-sign with you, here are a few other paths you can take:

Save up and pay cash: If you are disciplined enough and save enough money to pay upfront, this is a great option. This way you fully own your car and don't need to make monthly loan payments.

Ask your parents to loan you money: Your parents might be willing to give you a car loan as long as you promise to pay back the money over time. This way you can have a safe space to borrow and can earn their trust as a driver.

Work with your parents or other trusted adults: If you have an adult in your life willing to financially help with the purchase of your first car you might want to ask them to help by matching what you save. For example, if you have already saved up 3,000 dollars, they may be willing to match that.

BASIC AUTOMOTIVE SKILLS

It's very exciting to purchase your first car, however, there are a lot of responsibilities that come with this step toward freedom. This section will cover a lot of different scenarios that will help keep you and your vehicle safe and running.

Checking tire pressure and inflating tires— Your tires need to be properly inflated in order to keep the brakes working at their best. Your car may have a pressure light to let you know when the tires are getting low, so be sure you know what it looks like. If you don't have a pressure indicator built into your car, it is wise to keep a pressure gauge in your car at all times. To make sure you are checking the pressure properly, do so at least once each month.

Changing a tire and figuring out a blowout— Dealing with a blowout on the road can be pretty scary, so be sure you ask a parent or driving instructor about what to do when it happens. Changing a tire isn't a difficult process, just be sure you ask a trusted adult to show you how to do so before getting on the road. You will first need to know where your spare tire is, how to operate a jack (tool), how to remove your old tire, and how to replace it. It is best to have someone show you the exact process so you can feel comfortable if you ever need to do it in an emergency.

How to know when your car needs an oil change— A maintenance skill that a lot of new drivers forget about is figuring out when their car needs an oil change. If you have old oil or not enough, it will greatly affect how your car runs and its gas mileage. Cars usually need oil changes around every six months, but here are some other signs your car may need it:

- If your engine is making a hollow, knocking sound as you drive.
- Glowing warning lights called "check engine."
- Exhaust smoke coming from the exhaust pipe.
- If you drive a manual transmission car, you may have more trouble shifting gears.
- You hear a ticking sound coming from the engine.
- When idling, your car vibrates.

Jumpstarting a dead battery— When you experience a dead battery there are two crucial things to keep in mind: having a quality set of jumper cables kept in your car, and knowing the anatomy of your engine. You will need to clip your cables to those of another car. Here's a quick guidance tip that will help you remember: Red cables attach to the positive side, and black attaches to the negative. Again, it is a lot easier to become comfortable with this process if you have someone show you how to do it in front of you. So, be sure to ask a trusted adult to help you out.

Replacing your windshield wipers— Any amount of decreased visibility can make you feel a lot less confident. One of the best ways to make sure you can see the road clearly is to replace your windshield wipers when needed. This might occur when the water from rain doesn't properly come off or you can't seem to get rid of the dead bugs. You can purchase new windshield wipers and follow the instructions for replacement provided with the new set. When you successfully replace them, be sure to test them out a bit before getting back on the road.

How to react to the check engine light— The check engine light is a great tool because it is a warning sign that something is wrong with the engine, and typically catches all issues that may be going on. It can help you notice you need an oil change or a part replaced, or even alert you to a loose gas cap (the sealed space where you fill up your gas tank). If checking and changing your oil or gas cap doesn't fix the issue, you will need to head over to a mechanic. If your car has the check engine light on and is also making weird noises, producing odd smells, or vibrating when idling, be sure to see a mechanic to check out your car right away. Even further, scheduling routine maintenance checkups on a regular basis is another great way of making sure you don't encounter any problems.

CAR SERVICE & MAINTENANCE ICON SET

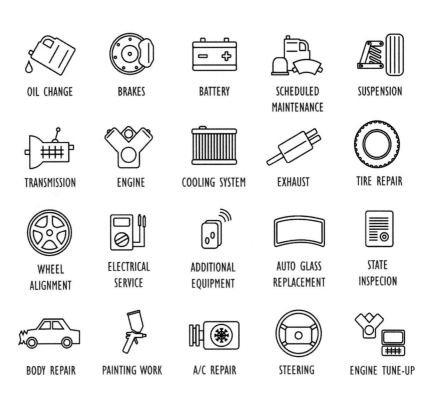

Everyone should be able to protect themselves and prevent dangerous situations from happening. In the next chapter, we will go over different safety skills and self-defense techniques.

CHAPTER 12
SAFETY SKILLS AND SELF-DEFENSE

Every teenage girl should be ready to protect herself, that is why there are so many tips and tricks in this chapter. Here we will cover street safety, situational awareness, basic self-defense, a guide to safe partying, internet safety, personal boundaries, and what you should do in an emergency. Let's jump right in!

BASIC STREET SAFETY TIPS

Knowing how to keep yourself safe and being prepared if you are attacked is an essential part of growing up. You should feel confident walking around knowing the tips below.

Situational awareness

Being situationally aware means being alert to your surroundings and the people around you. Being more aware can help prevent harm to yourself because you will have already seen the danger coming. This means that you will be able to escape attackers before they even target you, simply because you are aware of your surroundings.

Below are a few ways you can practice situational awareness:

- Drop any and all distractions— Even if it is more enjoyable, try not to walk around in public on your phone or with headphones on. When you are distracting your eyes and ears from sensing what is around you, your situational awareness drops significantly. This also means threats will see you as an easier target because you won't notice them coming toward you.
- Know your exit strategy— When you first enter a new room, building, party, concert, or other unfamiliar environment be sure to make a mental note of where the exits are. If an emergency were ever to happen, you would be able to get out much more quickly.
- Learn to position yourself wisely— A good habit to get into is standing near an exit (or where you can easily get to an exit) when you are in a new place or uncomfortable environment. Avoid putting yourself in a corner, middle of a crowd, somewhere you can't see an exit, or a place where you don't have a cell connection.
- Learn to scan your environment— When you're alone it can be easy to want to disappear and just look at the ground. But this makes you a much easier target and a lot more unsafe. Instead, make a habit of looking ahead and all around, at all times. Not necessarily in a super paranoid way, just in a way that you are present and aware of your space and what is going on at the moment.
- Start taking note of environmental hazards— When you get in the habit of simply being more aware of what is happening around you, you can prevent dangerous situations from occurring. This includes noticing potholes, hanging construction, weak trees, and traffic situations as you walk alone.

Preventing kidnaping

Kidnappers are getting smarter, and nowadays the most common way people get kidnapped is by being drawn into the kidnapper's car (even just down the street from the victim's house). Being street smart means practicing situational awareness alongside knowing the tricks most kidnappers use.

First off, never get near a stranger's car. Most of the time a kidnapper will work to get a woman or a child into their car, and once they do... it's game over. It is never appropriate for an adult who you don't know to ask you to come toward their car. If someone driving stops (or slows down) while you are walking and tries to start a conversation simply ignore them and keep walking. If they don't stop when you try to avoid them, or they stop their car and get out, immediately call your local first responders. On this call, tell them *exactly* where you are, where you are running toward, what the car looks like, what the person looks like, and what is happening.

As I mentioned before, kidnappers often use the same tricks to get people into their cars. Below is a table of the most common strategies they use:

The animal trick: When a person shows off or offers to give a person an animal.
The nice offer: This happens when someone offers a person or child candy, a ride, toys, or food.
The model trick: This trick is when a person pretends to be a model recruiter and promises success, fortune, and fame.
"I'm your parent's friend" trick: They will pretend that they were sent by your parents to pick you up.
Asking for help: The kidnapper will pretend to be lost and ask for directions, pretend to be looking for a lost animal, or will ask for help carrying something to their car.
"It's an emergency" trick: The kidnapper will pretend that a person or child's family member is in trouble and in the hospital and that they will take them there.

Here are four more tips for handling a dangerous situation with a possible kidnapper:

1. Walk or run in the opposite direction the car is going. This will give you a bit of extra time to find a safe spot to call emergency first responders.
2. Get to a place where you know a lot of people will be. This means taking the bigger, more well-known roads. So don't try to save time by going to a shortcut, because attacks are far less likely to happen when you are surrounded by other people.
3. Find good strangers. If you get lost, and can't find your house or your parents, go into a store and find someone with a name tag who works there. Don't run around yelling for help, because this will

make you even more confused. The person at the store will likely offer to help you find your parents, call them, or even call emergency responders. If anyone offers you a ride home, decline.
4. Memorize your information. Your parent's phone numbers, your home address, and the emergency number for your local area all need to be memorized so you can recite them in an emergency.

Basic self-defense

It can be scary to go out on your own, however, knowing how to defend yourself and being confident in your skills can make life a lot more comfortable. Taking a self-defense or martial arts class is definitely the best way to learn more self-defense skills, but below are some self-defense basics:

Control the distance— keeping yourself physically away from a possible attacker is the best way to prevent harm to yourself. From the beginning, show them that you are aware and will stay away from them, this gives you control over the situation. You can put space between you and an attacker in a few ways, including the following:

- Keeping yourself at least a leg's length away.
- Hold your arms out in front of you so you can push or bump the attacker if they get closer.
- Keep yourself moving and don't stop, regardless of whether the attacker stops or pursues you.
- Try to get an object between the two of you, such as a chair, table, corner of a building, or door.

Defending physical strikes and protecting yourself— The only time you will ever need to protect yourself from strikes is when you can't get away from an attacker. Start by getting your arms and elbows up to push away any strike that they might throw. Here are a few more tips to effectively defend yourself:

- When defending yourself get your attacker off balance by tripping them or pushing them. This will give you more space to run or land another strike.
- Keep your hands up, in front of your face.

- Hold your elbows tight to your body to protect your stomach and ribs.
- Keep moving. If you can't escape at least make sure you are a moving target, which is a lot harder to attack.

Setting a good fight stance and finding balance— A good (and effective) fight stance requires protection, just like we talked about with your arm positions, and balance. The balance for fighting back requires all of your body falling into line, and when one part of you is not aligned, you will be off balance. In order to find proper balance and a good fight stance you first need to make sure your head is upright and you can see your attacker at all times. Then, remember to widen your legs to be about shoulder-width apart. Always keep your knees slightly bent and your hips facing your opponent. Lastly, be sure to stand more on the balls of your feet so you can move as quickly as possible.

Breaking grips— If your attacker gets a hold of you, getting free will become your first priority. The main goal of breaking someone's grip on you is to find their weak points and attack them. Here are some tips to get someone off of you:

- Use both of your hands to break a grip, targeting the fingers (since they are the weakest point of someone's hold on you.
- If they have your wrists in their hands, roughly pull your arms toward the space where their fingers are.
- If they have your whole body lifted up, don't tense up and struggle, this will make it easier to carry you. Instead, relax your whole body and shake yourself. This will make you a lot harder to hold onto.

Travel Safety

If you are taking a trip to a new city or country, there are some important safety tips to keep in mind. Even if you won't be doing this solo for a while, knowing these skills is highly important.

Hide your wealth— You might be thinking, "I don't have much money," but the reality is that even an average westerner in a developing country will be considered rich. Just having a nice bag, jewelry, or watch can automatically make you the target of a crime. This means that your phone and wallet should always stay in a secure spot, and jewelry, watches, laptops, expensive purses, and nice shoes should all be left at your house or locked up in your hotel room.

Never appear lost— In general, it is good to try to never look like you are lost, scared, or completely alone. This especially applies when you are traveling. So, if you do get lost, don't pull out your map and look confused, instead go to a store or cafe, sit down, and figure it out there.

Read up on local crimes and danger zones— Online you will be able to find a lot of valuable information about common crimes, dangerous areas, and how to avoid danger. Before any trip you go on, be sure to do your research on what to avoid doing, common scams, the most frequent crimes, and areas you should avoid.

INTERNET SAFETY TIPS

We are in the digital age, and internet safety is equally as important as physical safety. Every teenage girl should know how to protect their privacy and how to not give personal information to strangers.

First, let's talk about how to keep your information safe online:

Start by creating strong passwords— When you create a password, be sure not to use a simple all-lowercase or numerical sequence. These are things that a hacker could easily figure out. In order to protect your personal information, be sure to use a mix of numbers and letters, uppercase and lowercase, as well as symbols. Even further, try not to use the same password every time you create a new account for something, because once one is hacked into, everything can be hacked.

Don't overshare on social media platforms— Don't be the person who shares every little detail of their life. Be especially careful if you are posting about a location while you are there. Be sure to set privacy so only people who you want to can view your posts, and to never share your daily routines or the places you frequent.

Be careful about free Wi-Fi— A lot of public Wi-Fi networks have very little security. This means that other people using the same network can easily access your personal online activity. So, if you are going to be using an online credit card, or working out private information, just wait until you're at home.

Check if a website is secure — Before you go to enter personal information, even just an email, but more importantly banking and credit card information, make sure the site is secure. You can do this by taking a look at the search bar and finding a lock symbol, or if you see an "https," before the URL. Both of these things mean the website is secure and won't release your personal information.

Take care with links and attachments — Online scammers can be really good, making legitimate-looking emails that appear to be from banks or other institutions. You can make sure a message or email is real by checking for spelling errors or a different email address than the actual user typically sends from.

Additional protection — You can secure your online information even further by installing anti-virus and anti-spy software alongside a firewall. You may even want to consider cyber insurance. Downloading a VPN is another great option so people can't track your location if they did get hold of your information.

Never tell a stranger your personal information— If someone reaches out to you saying you won something, are being recruited, or they're offering something in exchange for following a link or giving them your email, never give it. Even if it is a brand or company you recognize, sharing personal information over social media DM or text is never a good idea.

SAFE PARTYING

If you choose to go to parties as a teenager, you should know how to do so in a safe way. This section will go over how you can do that.

Risks at parties to be aware of

Going to parties can be a great way to socialize, get together with your friends, and have a fun time. But dangerous behavior can ruin it all, especially when drinking and drug usage comes into play. Below are some of the risks associated with drinking too much, and risky behavior you should be aware of before attending parties:

- Getting into a physical fight.
- Getting injured.
- Alcohol poisoning from drinking too much.
- Drug overdose.
- Driving after drinking and car accidents.
- Spiked drinks (where someone puts an unwanted drug or substance in your drink without permission).

Planning ahead

If you are planning to attend a party, the best way to make sure everything goes smoothly is to be sure to prepare. It can be hard to make decisions when you are already there and surrounded by other people, so the time to make choices is before the party even starts. Here are seven things to think about before you leave:

1. Arrange with a friend you trust to stay together. Ask this person to look out for you and offer to do the same. Go to the bathroom at the same time, watch each other's drinks, and make sure the other isn't going overboard with alcohol or substances.
2. Figure out how you are going to get home before you leave. You could keep some extra money to cover a taxi, arrange for a trusted person to come to pick you up, or have a friend who isn't drinking and will be responsible for driving you and others home. Also, be sure to have a plan B if the first doesn't work out. Maybe a sibling or other friend can come to pick you up if you can't call a taxi.
3. Be sure to eat a good meal before you go out. A full stomach can slow down the effects of alcohol.
4. If you are planning to drink, set a limit for yourself and stick to it.
5. The most effective way of avoiding problems with drugs is just to not use them. However, if you do, let a friend know, make sure you know what you are taking, and understand the risks involved.
6. Be sure you are aware of the laws in your area. Being drunk or drinking in public, especially if you are underage, can get you arrested.

Safe partying quick tips

When you do go out to a party there are some things you can keep in mind in order to keep yourself safe. So, while you're out:

- Pour your own drinks, and don't let others "top you off" because they may add way more alcohol than you wanted.
- Try your best to avoid taking shots or playing drinking games if you are worried about having too much. Things can get easily out of hand and too much alcohol can make you do dangerous things.
- Don't engage with people who are trying to start fights– just walk away.
- When you are reaching a point where you've had too much, you can pour yourself some water or a soft drink to occupy yourself and still sip on something.
- In order to avoid someone spiking your drink, either buy your own drink, drink out of a can or bottle, or watch closely as a someone

pours your drink. Even further, never set it down or leave it with someone you don't know or trust.
- Never try mixing alcohol and drugs, or even mixing kinds of drugs.
- Don't drive or get into a car with a driver who has been drinking.
- Remember that it is totally okay to say "no," don't let peer pressure force you into doing things you don't want to do. It's not that big of a deal and everyone will forget about it in the morning.
- Leave the venue if you aren't feeling safe.
- Don't take risks you normally wouldn't, such as jumping into a body of water you don't know the depth of.

PERSONAL BOUNDARIES

Setting boundaries and learning to say, "No," can be hard. But these personal boundaries you create can be used to keep yourself safe and out of situations you don't want to be in. Boundaries can be both physical and emotional and can be set with anyone in your life. They show others that you know your worth and that you can't be walked all over.

Setting personal boundaries can keep you from getting hurt in a romantic relationship, establish more independence at home, and get your friends to respect you more. It can be difficult to stand up for yourself, but when you learn to stand your ground you will be proud of yourself. Here are a few examples of healthy boundaries you can set:

- Letting a romantic partner know that you want things to move slowly with them. In a relationship, consent (making sure both people are on board) should be the basis of your interactions.
- Asking someone to stop teasing you about certain topics. And if they continue to do so, start spending less time with them. That means they don't respect your boundaries or your wishes.
- Telling a close friend that you do not want to drink, then asking for their support in your decisions.
- Asking your romantic partner to respect your time with other people by not getting jealous or texting and calling constantly.

- Discussing with a sibling or parent your need for alone time. This might mean requesting an hour or two each day when you can be in your room without interruptions.
- Telling a friend who always borrows money from you and never pays it back that you will not be offering them financial support anymore unless they can pay you back.

Healthy boundaries are a great habit to create. Now, let's discuss some examples of unhealthy boundaries and what you should not be doing if you want space from someone:

- Feeling like you can't trust anyone and choosing to shut everyone out of your life.
- Making your friends or romantic partners be there for you every single time you request, even if they have other responsibilities.
- Doing whatever your friends or romantic partners ask, even if you don't agree with it.
- Going against your beliefs and values in order to please other people, be liked, or fit in.
- Spending time with people who make you feel bad about yourself in order to feel like you belong.
- Letting things the people around you say be brushed under the rug.
- Letting romantic partners or friends decide what you do with your day or life.

Just as it is important for you to learn to set boundaries for yourself and to gain respect from the people around you, you also need to respect the boundaries of others. If you want people to respect you, make an effort to show them that you are going to respect their boundaries. This is the foundation of trust and healthy relationships.

Questions and Prompts For Your Personal Diary— Safety and Boundaries

1. How confident do you feel in your ability to stay aware and safe?
2. What steps do you plan to take in order to increase your personal and street safety?
3. Have you ever been nervous about going to a party? If so, why?
4. If you plan to go to parties, what tips are you planning on using? (Use this time to make a guide and checklist for yourself!)
5. What boundaries do you already have that you are upholding with the people around you?
6. Do you tend to be a people pleaser and let other people walk all over you?
7. What healthy boundaries are you going to start practicing this week?
8. Are there any unhealthy boundaries listed above that you participate in?

CHAPTER 13
GOAL-SETTING AND TIME MANAGEMENT

A massive part of developing independence and growing into an adult is learning time management and goal-setting skills. Anything you want to achieve in life will depend completely on how you set goals, what steps you take to achieve your goals, and how well you manage your time. It can be easy to think, "I have all the time in the world," and waste your teenage years not getting ready for adult life. But discovering how to properly organize your time and do what you have always wanted will be the key to your success as an adult!

SETTING REACHABLE GOALS

Simply setting a goal is not the same as creating *effective* and *reachable* goals. When you learn to set goals you will actively be developing a mindset that is focused on growth. Creating goals (and actually achieving them) is a great way of boosting your confidence, motivating yourself, learning about accountability and responsibility, and gaining better time organization skills. Below are some tips and exercises you can do to set realistic, achievable, and effective goals.

In order to set proper goals you need to know what you want and how to get there. Below are the top tips on how to set effective goals and reach them.

1. Set your big goal— This first step is actually where a lot of people fail. When you have too many big and broad goals you'll never be able to focus on reaching one. Here are a few ways you can get focused:

- Write out three of your biggest goals.
- Then, rank them in the order that you most want to achieve them.
- Now, ask yourself, "Which goal is going to be the most beneficial for me in the long run?" This can be based on how each will improve your happiness or well-being.

Now you know which one is most important to you, and this is the one you will focus your energy on first.

2. Try following SMART goal-setting when you are getting started:

S— Specific. Make sure your intentions are clear and well-defined.

M— Measurable. You need to be able to measure your progress and know that you have hit your goals.

A— Achievable. These goals need to be possible to reach.

R— Relevant. Are these goals you are setting relevant to your life? Are they within reach?

T— Timely. Successful goals have a clearly laid out deadline. This creates urgency and forces you to work hard.

3. Now, it's time to make a plan. List out the milestones that are standing between you and this future version of you. Maybe it's a job, saving your first 200 dollars, or setting aside time. The biggest key to this step is to create a clear roadmap that will get you to where you want to be. Essentially, you are setting smaller goals (that are easier to attain) in order to reach your big goals.

4. Answer these "W" questions in order to reach the goals you have set and create a better plan:

Who needs to be involved to help you achieve this goal?

What small steps do you need to reach first?

Where does this goal need to be reached? (If the goal is location-oriented.)

When do you want to achieve this goal?

Why do you even want to reach this goal?

5. Share your goals with the people around you so that they can help hold you accountable. You will be much more likely to reach a goal when you have told others about it. Even further, these people can help you reach your goals!

TIME MANAGEMENT TIPS

Now that you have set some goals it's time to learn to better manage your time. School, work, extra activities, and family life can all get overwhelming, so you are going to need to figure out how to handle it all. Some days it might feel like you don't have enough hours in the day to finish everything you need to, and that's when the following time management tips are helpful!

Journaling activity— tracking your days, weeks, and months

At the end of our days, weeks, and months, we should be able to list out pretty much everything we accomplished. This includes tasks, reached goals, and even meals we prepared. This is a great form to keep on hand to keep yourself on track to reach your goals!

Daily	What did you accomplish today?
	What are your goals tomorrow?
	Did you accomplish the goals you set for yourself today?
Weekly	What are the biggest things you were able to accomplish this week?
	What goals do you have for next week?
	What goals did you set for your week that you did not accomplish?
Monthly	What are your biggest goals for the next month?
	What are the highlights of your previous month?
	Did you reach all of the goals you set for yourself this month?

Break your big tasks into smaller ones

A big, daunting task can be overwhelming, which often leads us to put it off until the very last moment. You might feel like you have no idea where to start, and that is what causes the worst cases of procrastination.

When you have a big report due, but are tired after school or have other smaller assignments to complete, it can be easy to put it off until later. Why can't you just bring yourself to get started? The question you need to ask is: what does this big research report actually consist of?

- Research
- Gather your sources
- Make an outline
- Start a rough draft
- And finalize your paper

No wonder you are having a hard time just writing your paper. It isn't really just one task. In order to manage your time well, break up your big and overwhelming tasks into smaller ones that you can spread out over the course of days or weeks. The same thing goes for cleaning your room and studying for tests.

Make a list of priorities

When you have a lot of different tasks to complete, it can be hard to pick somewhere to begin. This is when you need to pioritze certain things to finish first and choose others that can wait a little bit. You can create this list in just a few simple steps:

1. Write out everything you need to get done that day (or week).
2. Highlight or underline in *red* the tasks that are urgent and need to be finished rather quickly.
3. Next, highlight or underline in *yellow* what would be nice to get done soon, but isn't urgent.
4. Lastly, these are the tasks you can put off until the end of the day or week. Highlight or underline these in *green.*

Now you have your to-do list arranged in order of what *needs* to be done first. Having this list will give you a start and end point! This will additionally help you organize your time and get things done when they need to be finished.

Get prepared for school the night before

The morning rush to get to school, forgotten lunch, messy hair, lost homework papers, and tardiness can all be avoided by simply planning a few things the night before. Odds are, you have an extra fifteen to thirty minutes to spare just before bedtime to plan your outfit and pack your lunch. So, here are some ways you can optimize your morning, forget nothing, and be on time:

- Pack your lunch the night before. Even if you are just bagging fruits and vegetables and making a sandwich, it saves you precious time in your morning.
- Prepare your homework, papers, and supplies. A good habit to get into is making a list of everything you need to turn in the next day as well as any supplies you may need. When you pack everything the night before you won't even need to waste time checking it in the morning.

- Picking out outfits can be a really big time-sucker (especially if you don't wear uniforms). So, do your whole morning routine of digging through your closet and trying everything on the night before. That way you won't be stressed about it when you wake up! A great tip is to check your weather app for the following day so you know what temperatures to dress for.

Use a planner

A great way to learn time management is by practicing using a planner. You can either do this with a traditional journal or download an agenda app on your phone. With a planner, you will be able to note down anything you need to get done the day before, check things off, prioritize tasks, and plan out your week.

Having everything written down in one place will help keep you organized and on time. You will know exactly what to expect from your days and weeks, as well as what you need to turn in at school, projects you need to finish, and extracurricular activities!

Tips to avoid procrastination

Procrastination is the biggest enemy of time management. Whether you are putting off writing an essay or scrolling social media when you should be doing homework, there are things you can do to help you stop procrastinating and keep yourself on task:

- Time yourself— A great way to get something done in a shorter time frame is to set an alarm, focus, and get down to work. You don't need to commit to hours of work and can break your tasks up into smaller pieces. One effective way of doing this is by setting fifteen or twenty-minute timers, working on something for that time, taking a break, then repeating.
- Remove distractions— Phones, television, books, music, and people can all be really good distractions. So, if you find yourself procrastinating by scrolling on your phone or chatting with a friend, try to remove those distractions for a small period of time while you focus.

- Reward yourself— When you have the incentive to get something done you will be far less likely to procrastinate. For example, you can take a break, grab a snack, or watch a television show each time you finish a task. If you need more of a push, you could even tell yourself to read two or three pages of your textbook, then you can have a piece of candy or take a small break. Whatever keeps you going is what you should use!
- Tell someone your goals— Having someone else to hold you accountable for focusing or completing your work makes you a lot more likely to actually get things done. You can tell your parents or a friend that you are going to study for thirty minutes, or that you need to finish a paper that night. And have them check in on you to make sure you are actually doing what you promised yourself.
- Complete your tasks in an order that inspires you— This might mean doing the easiest things first to prepare for the harder ones. Or it might mean getting your most difficult tasks out of the way first. Whatever it is, make sure you are feeling ready to take on what comes next.
- Figure out when you have the most energy— Some people work best in the morning and then can't bring themselves to focus at night. Others can't work in the morning but have laser focus in the afternoons or at night. When you don't have energy, you will be much more likely to procrastinate. So, take note of when you feel most energized and inspired to complete your tasks and try to work at those times.

> **Questions and Prompts For Your Personal Diary— Goals and Time Management**
>
> 1. What are three goals you want to reach by the time you graduate high school?
> 2. What is your number one goal?
> 3. What are you going to start doing *this week* to achieve your goals?
> 4. Do you feel that you are already good at managing your time? If so, what skills are you going to keep using? If not, which of the above skills will you start using?
> 5. Describe when you tend to procrastinate the most. How do you feel after?
> 6. What tips are you going to start using to fight this procrastination?

Organizing your time, energy, and tasks is highly important for reaching your goals. But what is organization without physical tidiness and an organized space? Your room might feel like a disaster, but you don't even want to touch it. In the next chapter, we will talk all about why it is important to keep your things neat, and how you can organize your room, backpack, and items to make your life a whole lot easier!

CHAPTER 14
ORGANIZATIONAL SKILLS

There are actually more benefits to being organized than just being able to find your things. When you have a disorganized space, you can experience more stress and have less concentration. In fact, students who lack organizational skills experience more academic challenges, have lower grades, and even have more negative perceptions and interactions with teachers (Hanson, 2023). Even the smallest improvements in practices of decluttering and organization can mean better time management, better ability to focus, and a more positive school experience. But how do you even get started?

Your first step in learning to keep your things more organized is to take note of areas where you need to clean up more. Use the chart below to note down if these places are organized or could use some cleaning up:

Space:	Is it neat or messy?
Your room	
Your backpack	
Locker at school	
Desk at home or school	
School folders (holding assignments)	
Your planner or calendar	
Your computer's files (in organized categories)	
The tabs of your computer	

Now that you have taken note of your strongest and weakest points, it's time to discover some tools to organize your spaces.

START DECLUTTERING

The best way to start cleaning your spaces and organizing your things is to begin decluttering. To start this process you are going to need a trash can, bag, or box to put items in. You can declutter your room, locker, desk, and backpack—basically any place you feel is disorganized..

Now, you are going to create four piles for your items to go in:

Trash— For the items you no longer need, that are worn, damaged, or can't be passed on to someone else.

Donation— This is for things you no longer need or use that are still in good condition that you can donate or give to family or friends.

Storage— For the items you want to keep but don't need direct access to. This includes keepsakes, pictures, and seasonal items like clothes and shoes.

Organize— This pile will be the things you want to keep and need access to on a regular basis. These things will then be organized in specific places.

From here, you are going to focus on one space at a time. Maybe you'll start with your backpack, a drawer, shelves, or desk, then move on to the rest of your room. When you are going through the process of decluttering it is important to ask yourself the right questions when deciding where each item goes. So, ask yourself:

"Do I really need this item anymore?"

"Have I used this item within the last three to six months? And when was the last time I used it?"

"Have I outgrown this?"

"Do I still use this item or is it just taking up space?"

DESIGNATED PLACES

After you have effectively decluttered your space, you will likely be left with a lot more room to give your items their own place. So, designating specific places for each item will be the key to putting your space back together. This technique means finding the right place for each thing so you can find it efficiently and put it back where it goes without a problem. You can even take a photo of everything and where it goes so you can reorganize your things again from time to time. Your designated spaces might look like this:

- Bedtime items going on your nightstand, and nothing else.
- Morning routine tools and items go on your vanity or bathroom counter.
- School supplies stay on your desk or in your backpack.
- Your phone charger stays in the same place.
- A hanger on the back of your door for your backpack, purse, and keys.

GO ONE AREA AT A TIME— LEARNING TO DIVIDE AND CONQUER

It can be overwhelming to look at a messy room and have no clue where to start. If you can't even imagine getting started on organizing your spaces and items then it's time to learn to divide and conquer. You don't need to clean your whole room in one session. You also don't need to "just start." Here are some strategies you can use to split up the work and make it less daunting to get started:

- Start by picking a corner or area of your room to focus on. This might be your closet, desk, vanity, shelves, bedside table, or drawers.
- Set a timer for yourself and focus all of your energy on decluttering and organizing just that space. When the time is up, let yourself take a break.
- If you need more time to get this area done, set another timer and repeat until you are happy with the result.

- Now, move to another area of your room and repeat the same process. Before you know it, you will have gone through your entire room!

If you are still feeling overwhelmed, I have a different strategy for you. These steps are a specific order of tasks you can complete to get your room clean:

1. Pick up everything off the floor. Anything that needs to go in the trash needs to be thrown away as well.
2. Take out the trash.
3. Put all of your dirty clothes in the hamper and take them to the washing machine.
4. Put away all clean clothes.
5. Clear off any surfaces that are cluttered with items that don't belong.
6. Wipe off all surfaces.
7. Organize the items you picked up and put them in their designated spaces.

> **Questions and Prompts For Your Personal Diary— Brainstorming Organizational Ideas**
>
> 1. What areas of your life do you feel need more organization?
>
> 2. What tips from this chapter are you going to start using this week?
>
> 3. What is one thing you can clean today that would clear your space?

In the next chapter we will go over how you can go about applying for your first job, what to do in interviews, and how to uphold a good standard of work. It's an exciting thing to be able to start making money! Let's jump right in!

CHAPTER 15
GETTING A JOB AND KEEPING IT

Beginning the search for your first job is both scary and exciting at the same time. Finding a job is hard for anyone. Period. When you don't have workplace experience, have never been to a job interview, or even written a resume, it can be even more daunting. But, rest assured, this chapter will be your guide on how to search for a job, write a resume, get an interview and *nail it*, and what to do when you actually start!

TIPS TO PREPARE TO GET YOUR FIRST JOB

Alright, it's time to get ready for the job hunt. But where do you even start? Before you go out and offer your services you are going to need a solid, yet simple, resume. This can be very confusing to put together, especially if you have never had a job before, so here are a few tips for what you should put on your first resume:

- Any and every freelance job you have had (such as babysitting, snow shoveling, and lawn mowing) as well as the contact of the person you worked for.
- A leadership position you held in school or in an extracurricular activity. This will show that you can take charge and have good character.

- Any academic recognitions and achievements you may have.
- School projects or advanced courses that show discipline or leadership.
- Involvement in school clubs, art, dance, or music lessons, and even participation in sports.
- Any volunteer experiences you may have.
- Expand on any experiences you have that highlight your dedication, discipline, or leadership. Employers are going to be looking to hire teens who are mature and ready to handle anything that comes their way.
- Be sure you include your contact information as well (email and phone number).

Don't be intimidated if you don't have much to put on your resume, this is a first job, after all. Just be sure you make it look clean and put together, as well as error-free.

Looking for leads

Networking (or connecting with the people around you naturally) is always a great way of finding leads for jobs. You truly never know who might have an opportunity, or know someone who does, that fits you perfectly! To get started networking and looking for jobs within your network, simply reach out to some friends who already have jobs and ask about their experience. What are their responsibilities? How is the manager? Is it a good place to work? If all sounds good, you can them ask if they are hiring and to have an introduction to their supervisor.

A few other ways you can use networking to look for a job include:

- Ask your parents if they have any contacts with local businesses that are looking to hire.
- Reach out to people you have done small jobs for and ask if they know anyone looking for long-term employees.
- Reach out to other trusted adults in your life including teachers, neighbors, coaches, and counselors asking if they have any local job opportunities in mind.

When you start getting recommendations and suggestions for places to apply, it's time to make a list of all of your possibilities. Of course, you can still apply at places where you don't have contacts but you know are hiring as well. With that list, you will then arrange a meeting with a supervisor or walk in and offer your resume.

Getting ready for the interview

The next step is getting ready for the interviews. Please note that if you choose to apply in person there is a possibility that you will be asked to interview right then and there. So, all of these tips can be applied to how you act and present yourself when you bring your resume to an employer in person.

So, what do you even wear to an interview? As a general rule of thumb, make sure your outfit is something your grandmother would approve of you wearing. You don't need to be overdressed, just be appropriate and tidy. This includes not wearing shorts, flip-flops, worn-out shoes, or dirty clothes. Even further, don't wear a hat, and make sure your phone is put away and switched to silent.

When you go to an employer and ask for the job, your outfit will matter less than the confidence you show. So, when you walk through that door, keep your chin up and your posture straight, have a firm handshake, and maintain eye contact. This confidence is something employers look for when they are hiring.

Part of having confidence when you apply or when you have an interview is being fully prepared. There are some very common questions interviewers will ask, and they have common expectations of what they want to hear from you. So, here are a few questions that you can prepare to answer ahead of time:

"Why are you looking for a job?"— Obviously everyone wants to make money from a job. But they really want to know if you are interested in the field and if your passions align with the work.

"What makes you interested in working with this company?"— They want to know if you have done your research and really know what their company is and stands for.

"Tell me about yourself." — No, they don't want to know that you have a pet dog. They actually want to know about your interests, academic accomplishments, and strengths as a person.

"What accomplishment are you most proud of?" — You shouldn't brag too much, they really just want to know about your qualities and strengths.

"How would you describe your teamwork abilities?" — In this question, employers want to know if you are a good fit for a position with other employees or if you'd be better for something more independent.

"Why should we hire you?" — This one can be scary to answer, but the employer just wants to know what you have to offer them as an employee.

However, sometimes things don't work out, and even if you thought you handled everything perfectly, you might not get the job. So, you are also going to need to prepare yourself for rejection. If you do end up getting a rejection there are proper ways you can respond. These include:

"Well, if you are looking for someone like me in the future, make sure to give me a call. I will leave a copy of my resume."

"Thank you for your time, if you change your mind or find me a good fit for your company in the future I will leave my contact information and resume."

These responses can be surprising to employers and show them that you really are serious about their company and securing a job there.

Following up

So, you've made it through the interview, now what do you do? Following up with an employer after a job interview can actually be one of the most important steps in getting a job. This is because employers see candidates who follow up as willing and ready to participate, take responsibility, and are dedicated to the job. So, always be sure to make a follow-up call or email to get in touch and see where they are at in the hiring process.

Even further, don't be afraid to get out of your comfort zone and go to the establishment in person. Showing this level of enthusiasm will increase their confidence if they are considering hiring you.

NOW IT'S TIME TO WORK HARD

The application and interview process is just the beginning. Once you have secured a job, there are a few things that you need to keep in mind. The tips below will be your keys to success at your new job and help you thrive, do a good job, and keep your position.

- Dress for success every day— If you are going to be wearing a uniform at your job, dressing well doesn't just mean putting the bare minimum effort in. It means making sure your uniform is neat, clean, and free of wrinkles when you head to work. However, if there isn't a uniform you still need to practice dressing appropriately. Oftentimes, workplaces will have a dress code, but if not keep it clean and professional. So, your best bet will be to wear clothes that are clean, simple, and fit well, with no tattered shoes or clothes, and a tidy hairstyle.
- Handling grumpy customers with grace— If you are working any sort of part-time job as a high schooler, odds are you will encounter customers who are less than pleasant. Just remember, even if this isn't *actually* true, you should work your job with the saying, "The customer is always right," as your motto. Even if the people you are dealing with are not being rational, it is now your job to be the voice of reason. So fix anything that they viewed as wrong and bring your supervisor in when necessary. Most of the time these people aren't even being realistic, but that is not your problem to argue about.
- Separate your personal problems from your work life— Teens are naturally very social, and it might be really tempting to rant about your personal problems to a co-worker or manager but (unless they are your friend), this is not the time or place. Even more, if an argument arises at work *with* a co-worker, be sure to handle it privately, without roping your boss or manager in. This attitude of diffusing situations and not complaining will show your superiors that you have a positive effect on the workplace.
- Behave as a professional with all co-workers and supervisors— Entry-level jobs and part-time jobs will often be full of hard-to-handle co-workers and sometimes difficult managers. When

someone at work is having a bad attitude with you, this is not a time to correct them or disrespect them, since even this could get you out of your job. Behaving with professionalism in your job means respecting even the people who don't respect you, and doing your tasks even if the people around you won't do theirs.
- Never leave work early, arrive late, or skip work without prior approval from a superior. It won't be hard to ask someone to cover you, just don't leave or bail without letting your managers and co-workers know beforehand.
- It's time to unplug— The moment you arrive at work you need to switch off your phone and be present and ready to do your job. Either leave your phone on mute or tuck it away so you won't be tempted to look at it. Your employer is not paying you to sit on your phone and scroll all day. So, only use your phone in emergencies or if you are on a designated break.
- It is important to keep a positive attitude— A first job might be boring or hard to handle at times, but if you manage to develop a good attitude your days will finish faster. Even further, showing enthusiasm and a good attitude will potentially offer promotions and higher pay. This can be seen in showing up on time and when you are scheduled, meeting all expectations of you, and bringing a positive vibe to the workplace. Also, a positive voice in a workplace has the potential to calm down arguments with other co-workers and customers.
- Lastly, when it's time to move on from a job— Before you walk out the door there are some things you should remember:

  ○ Give a two-week notice.

  ○ Talk about your plans, and when you are looking to leave, in advance with a manager.

  ○ Be sure to thank your boss for the job and the opportunity.

  ○ Leave on a positive note.

  ○ Stay in contact and have good relations with your employer, this way they may serve as a future contact and reference.

Practical home skills are another group of highly important tools every young person should learn and develop. The next chapter will be all about how to manage a home, cook, sew, and practically live on your own in the future.

CHAPTER 16
PRACTICAL HOME SKILLS

Soon you will be on your own and have to manage yourself and a place of your own. This means that everything your parents or guardians did for you will become your responsibility. The skills covered in this chapter are critical for any teen and budding young adult to learn in order to successfully live on their own.

MANAGING A HOME— DOMESTIC SKILLS

Managing a home is about a lot more than just cooking and cleaning. Organization, lists, and cleaning strategies are all super important skills you will need to develop in order to live successfully alone. Below are some great domestic skills and strategies you can start learning while you live at home with your parents.

Checklists and to-do lists

Keeping a home and your life organized can be overwhelming at times. You will slowly learn to create your own systems, but a great place to begin is with checklists and to-do lists. There are so many things that come up that you will need to remember a week, or even a month later. Life will go on, you might need to fix something or pick up your car, and then forget everything else you need to dothat day. However, if you create weekly and daily to-do lists (organized in order of urgency) you don't need to have those tasks taking up space in your brain.

Cleaning routines

Some cleaning skills will need to be done on a daily basis, and others weekly or monthly. Keeping up with these tasks and creating a cleaning schedule and routine will mean the difference between manageable cleaning and an overwhelming mess. So, it's time to sit down and make a list of the chores that you need to do (even if it just applies to your bedroom) in order to get into the habit of using a cleaning routine. Below is an example of the different chores you will need to be doing and how they may be spilt up.

Daily chores may include:

- Making your bed.
- Watering plants that need it daily.
- Cleaning the kitchen counters after use.
- Washing dishes.
- Sweeping or vacuuming the floors.
- Washing your dirty clothes.
- Sorting through your school papers at the end of the day.
- Organizing the bathroom after use.
- Anything that can be done relatively quickly and will help keep your space clean and organized.

Weekly chores may include:

- Mopping and vacuuming the whole house (or space).
- Dusting flat surfaces.
- Deep cleaning the bathroom.
- Changing bedsheets.

Monthly chores may include:

- Deep clean bedroom.
- A monthly clean of your dishwasher and laundry machine.
- Dust the ceiling fans and blinds.

- Check the furnace or AC filters.

If you can successfully break up your chores into different categories, you will be able to keep your space clean without having to spend a full weekend doing everything. Consistently doing a little at a time and sticking to a schedule that works for you will be the key to a clean and organized home.

Using a calendar

When you live on your own you are going to need to remember every appointment, meeting, and activity that you have to go to. You are likely going to be trying to remember a hundred other things at the same time, and tasks might slip through the cracks. Getting into the habit of using a calendar or planner on a regular basis will be extremely beneficial. Once you are used to automatically putting items on your calendar, you will just need to check what's on the schedule for the day and continue on. This will eliminate all of those guessing games and help you feel far less stressed. You don't need to carry around a planner or even have a physical calendar if that's not your thing. There are plenty of online versions that can be just as handy.

Laundry

There is no escaping washing your clothes, so it's essential to learn how to do it in an efficient and easy-to-manage manner. Below are the steps for managing your laundry and properly cleaning your clothes:

1. Sort your items— You will first need to separate your light and dark-colored clothes. If you wash these together, your colored clothes can ruin your whites. Even further, whites should be washed in hot or warm water to ensure the best cleaning.
2. Check the care label— Reading the label on your clothes is a crucial part of doing laundry if you don't want your clothes to shrink or change colors. The label will recommend a cold wash, warm wash, or gentle wash, just to name a few specifications.
3. Don't overload your cycle— Putting too many clothes in the washer can be a good way of making sure your clothes don't come out fully cleaned. You don't just want to get them wet, you want the detergent to reach every item, and this won't happen if your load is too full.

4. Drying— Delicate clothes and ones that are likely to shrink should be hung up to dry, rather than being put in the dryer. This will help extend the life of your clothes and protect them from being ruined.

COOKING AND FOOD

Learning how to cook can be a daunting task, but with the right shopping and prep skills, you can learn to create nutritious meals with ease. Discovering cooking skills is an essential part of managing a home because takeout and fast food will not be the best options (for your body or your wallet.) Below are some tips on how you can learn to cook and manage your shopping when you leave the house!

Meal prepping and planning

Meal prep is a true secret weapon that can be your key to success in the kitchen. It will save you hours every day and defeat the daily struggle of deciding what to cook for dinner when you have a bunch of other things you need to worry about. Meal planning also helps:

- Reduce the amount of time you spend at the store and the number of trips you need to take.
- It will save you money in the long run because you know to buy just what you are prepping for the week. This cuts down on impulse purchases and helps you stick to a budget.
- It will help you save money on takeout and fast food because you will always have something ready and healthy at home.
- You will be able to eat healthier since meal-prepped food often includes cooked vegetables, beans, cooked meats, and rice.

Here are some easy steps you can follow to start meal prepping!

1. Take a look at your upcoming week. What do you have scheduled on the calendar? What nights will you be too busy to cook? Will you be going out to eat at all? This will help you schedule easy-to-warm-up meals on the days you will be the busiest.
2. Now, make a list of what you *usually* eat for breakfasts, lunches, and snacks. It is common for people to eat a lot of the same things

throughout the day and seek variety at dinner time. These are the first meals you are going to plan since they will likely be the easiest.
3. Make a list of dinner ideas you want throughout your week. When you have your ideas, all you need to do is schedule them out to make the most sense throughout your week.
4. It's now time to create a grocery list! You can organize this list into meats, dairy, vegetables and fruits, snacks, cereals and bread, and extras.
5. From here you will need to decide if you want to cook each night for dinner or prep your ingredients. You can pre-cook vegetables, rice, meat, sauces, and noodles to be reheated at a later time in the week.

Basic cooking skills

When you are first starting your cooking journey there are some basic skills that will come in handy for the rest of your life. Below is a list of the best cooking skills you can start developing today!

- Learning to cook eggs— An essential cooking skill is discovering different ways to cook eggs. They are a saving grace to add protein to any meal and can go with most sides. Poached, fried, on toast, scrambled, hard-boiled, etc. There are so many ways to eat eggs!
- A quick and easy pasta dish— Pasta is a relatively cheap and easy meal you should have on hand. It is also great because you can create so many different sauces to go with it. Having a go-to pasta dish you can whip up in no time will come in handy.
- Cooking meat— Learning to cook meat is a highly important skill to learn. While some meats like beef and lamb can be served a little rare or pink, chicken and pork need to be cooked all the way through.
- A basic salad or vegetable dish— Knowing ways you enjoy eating vegetables, and figuring out how to make them one of your specialties will be a great skill to have. So, take some time to experiment with different salads and cooked vegetable dishes to find what you can practice and nail!
- Smoothies— You might find yourself in a rush and needing to eat breakfast on the go, so a smoothie can be a great way to get your fruits and some protein in as you run around. Find one really good

smoothie (preferably with a protein source such as greek yogurt or protein powder) and revert to that when you might not have enough time for a sit-down breakfast.
- Finding new recipes— You can look around for healthy, yummy, and easy meals. There are plenty of apps, cookbooks, and websites that offer simple recipes that you can learn to add to your weekly cooking.
- Discover something you like to bake— Baking is a really handy skill to have. Whether it's a bread recipe or some cookies, baked goods last a while and can be something nice to have on hand.
- Rice— If you don't have a rice cooker then learning to cook rice in a pot is something you may need to practice. Rice is a great, healthy, cheap, and filling food that you can add to a lot of different meals.
- Healthy and easy snacks— Figuring out quick and easy healthy snacks will be a good way to cut down on your grocery budget and fast food. These may include things like carrots and hummus, popcorn, or homemade trail mix.

Tips for grocery shopping

Even if you know how to cook, grocery shopping is a whole other skill you will soon need to master. Finding strategies to shop and eat healthier, as well as save some money will start in the grocery store. Here are some of the best tips to save money and shop in a better way:

- Create a list and stick to it. This will help you to not buy things you don't need and keep you in the mindset of healthy eating if that is what you already planned for.
- Don't grocery shop when you're hungry. If you do this you will likely find yourself reaching for more snacks, unhealthy foods, and things that sound good at the moment. However, if you weren't hungry you probably wouldn't have grabbed those foods.
- Cook around coupons— If you see coupons for pasta, a certain fruit, or a vegetable, be sure to shop based on the discounts you have found. This will save some money and help keep you on track in the grocery store.

- Sign up for the loyalty program— It might sound annoying to sign up, but if you frequent the same grocery stores, signing up for their discount and loyalty programs can really help save some money.
- Buy the generic version— Oftentimes generic and name-brand items taste the same, but the branded ones are usually a lot more expensive. If you are able to find different and cheaper versions of your favorite products, opt for the less expensive options.
- Buy in bulk— Oats, cereals, nuts, and other items that don't spoil are great to buy in large quantities. If you are able to find a discounted price for something you know you'll be using a lot, go for it!

In the next chapter, we will be talking about problem-solving skills. Again, you are budding into a young adult, and finding ways to logically solve problems on your own will be crucial to your success. These skills will be important in daily life, school, and your future career.

CHAPTER 17
PROBLEM-SOLVING SKILLS

Things can't go according to plan every time. Your parents and the other adults around you will be doing the majority of the problem-solving for you right now, but when you are on your own you will need the skills to figure things out by yourself. There are six simple steps you will need to learn to become successful at problem-solving. In this chapter, we will cover each of these steps as well as some exercises you can do to practice these skills on your own.

WHAT ARE PROBLEM-SOLVING SKILLS?

Problem-solving skills are just what they sound like. These skills help you to identify a problem, discover the root cause, find an effective solution, and put that solution into action. Even further, problem-solving skills will help you evaluate how successful your strategies were.

The best problem-solvers are actually able to identify problems before they become too big, find ways to fix them, and lessen the impact that any issues would have had. The two keys to problem-solving are logic and creativity. You need to be able to look at a situation with clear eyes to see the problems, then use your imagination to create inventive solutions.

If you have strong problem-solving skills you will find more success in school and work, and find new and innovative ways to achieve your goals. Here are some of the other skills you will be likely to use when solving a problem:

- Imagination
- Brainstorming
- Analysis
- Research skills
- Decision-making
- Planning skills
- Leadership
- Organization
- Judgment
- Patience
- Communication
- Initiative (making the first moves)
- Goal setting
- Open mindedness
- Teamwork

SIX STEPS TO SOLVING A PROBLEM

1. Find the problem

The first step to solving a problem is figuring out what the issue really is. If you are working with other people, this step will help get everyone to understand what you are struggling with. When you have a problem that you understand, you are actually making it a *solvable* problem.

The key here is to think calmly and clearly. What is it you are having hardship with? What is happening because of this problem? Here are some examples of clearly expressed problems:

I was invited to two events at the same time on the same day, and I cannot go to both.

My sister and I are always arguing over using each other's things.

I have three big assignments due tomorrow and haven't started on any of them.

I want to go to a party tomorrow but don't have anyone to drive me.

2. Find the root issue (Why is this a problem?)

So now you know *what* the problem is. Now it's time to figure out what the root cause is and *why* it's a problem in the first place. You can answer these questions below to discover where these feelings and problems are coming from:

Why is this problem even important to me?

Why do I need this?

What is the worst-case scenario?

What do I really think is going to happen as an outcome?

How did this problem start?

What am I feeling about this situation? (Create a list of different emotions you are experiencing).

Use this step to figure out if the problem at hand really is as important as you may think. By the end of answering the questions above you will have a good idea of what you are dealing with and how important the issue really is.

3. Brainstorm possible solutions

This next step will be all about imagining any and every possible solution to your problem. They don't even need to make sense, you just need a range of possible options to choose from. Funny, extreme, and reasonable solutions are all welcome here. Below are a few examples of kinds of solutions you could write down:

I buy two of every piece of clothing I own so it won't bother me if my sister takes one. (Crazy or not, you can list *any* possible solution).

My sibling and I create a schedule for when we use the television.

I can start on one project, finish it, then move on to the next.

I can ask a friend to pick me up for the party or take a cab.

I choose to go to the first event for the first half, and the next event for the second half.

4. Pros and cons— Evaluation

Now it's time to narrow down the solutions that are actually possible. Look at every possible solution that you brainstormed and create a pros and cons list for each. This process will help you to recognize which solutions can't happen, and decide which will make the most sense. When you see a solution that would take too much time and energy, or just wouldn't actually work, you can cross it off your list of possibilities.

From here you have all of the good and bad sides of each option. You can now go through your list and rate each solution from one to ten (ten being the best, taking the least time and energy, and having the best possible outcome).

5. Make a decision and put it into action

Now you need to make a decision. Now that you have your pros and cons and have ranked each possibility, your choice will be much easier than it was three steps ago. In the decision-making process, you will need to compare the pros and cons lists that you have compiled and make an informed choice.

Once you have made your decision it's time to put it into action. In order to do this you are going to need to plan out exactly the steps you are going to take to create your desired outcome. To start creating a plan, answer the questions below:

Who needs to be involved?

What will each person's role be?

What do you need to put this plan into action? (For example: time, resources, help, energy, etc.)

What is the first step you need to take to get started with your plan?

When you know what it will take to put this decision into action, it's time for you to take the necessary steps to move forward. It is important to remember that your desired outcome will not become your reality if you don't work to make it happen. So, throughout the process, you will need to check in on how things are going, what needs to be changed, and if the other people are doing their part.

6. Review the outcome

Not every solution will work out. Even the most well-thought-out ideas can have their flaws or bring a different end result. This means that by the time you should be seeing your end goals you should take some time to review your actions and change up your process if necessary. This is an essential piece of effectively solving a problem. Sometimes things will not go as planned so you will need to learn how to adapt to your situations. Here are some questions you can ask yourself when you go to evaluate your solution's outcome:

What went according to plan?

What worked well?

What didn't work well or go according to the plan?

What could you have done differently to make the process smoother?

Did you reach the end goal that you wanted? If not, how can you move forward from here?

If your chosen solution didn't work at all, you will need to go back to the first step and do this process again. It may take a few tries to get to where you want to be, but if you stick to this process you will get there!

THE ENEMIES OF PROBLEM-SOLVING SKILLS

There are a few roadblocks you may encounter when trying to find solutions to your problems. Here are a few common complications that may be holding you back from becoming a powerful problem-solver:

Misreading the situation— Misdiagnosing the situation due to wrong judgments and perceptions can make every step in the process above much more difficult. You need to be able to clearly look at what you are facing, what challenges you need to overcome, and define what you are dealing with. If you aren't careful, you may end up wasting time on solutions that don't address the root cause of your problem.

Communication barriers— This simply means that you need to get everyone on the same page before even brainstorming possible situations. If you want to be successful when problem-solving with a team you may need to acknowledge that you don't have all the answers and may have a limited understanding of the situation at hand. You must not presume that you know more than the others on the team, and you need to let the others know that they also may have a limited understanding. You may even need to let others know that you have valuable input by communicating your ideas in a more clear way.

Lacking empathy— A key part of problem-solving, especially with a group of other people, is being empathetic. Every problem and solution is connected to human emotions and abilities, or lack thereof. You must recognize that other people are likely affected by this problem and that people may be affected by your possible solutions. A truly successful solution will be considerate of everyone involved, directly or indirectly.

Solution bias— There is no single correct way of thinking, and there will not be one universal solution that will work for every problem. If you think there is, it may just be a bandage that covers the problem, rather than something that heals it. If you want to effectively solve problems, you will need to look at each individual problem without forcing a pre-existing solution into action. You must keep yourself from jumping to conclusions without assessing all possibilities. Just remember that it is better to have a long-lasting solution that takes time to develop than a quick solution that doesn't really work.

EXERCISES TO INCREASE PROBLEM-SOLVING SKILLS

There are other ways you can practice the skills that are required to be a good problem-solver. Below are some activities and exercises you can practice to hone your skills:

- Coding for teens— There are many online resources for free coding practice for teens. If you are into computer coding this could be a great way to practice going through the process of programming something.

- Crossword puzzles— These puzzles can be really fun and also work to encourage using context clues as well as the process of elimination.
- Jigsaw puzzles— A great way to practice ordering and taking the right steps forward is by doing a good old-fashioned puzzle!
- Sudoku— This kind of puzzle will challenge you to compare different possibilities and test different options. You will need to discover an organized approach if you want to be successful.
- Debate club— Healthy debates are all about looking at things from different angles, which is an essential problem-solving skill. You will need to self-analyze, listen to opposing sides, and create a plan of action on how you will argue in effective ways.

> **Questions and Prompts For Your Personal Diary— Reflection**
>
> 1. When was the last time you experienced a problem you couldn't solve? If you had the skills above, do you think you would have encountered the same troubles?
> 2. What are the most common struggles you experience? How do you normally go about solving these problems?
> 3. What problem-solving skills above do you think you need to work on the most? (i.e: decision-making, evaluation, etc.)

Next up, you are off to the final chapter! In the next section, we will talk about how you can gain more independence and develop yourself as an individual.

CHAPTER 18
FINDING A SENSE OF INDEPENDENCE AND DEVELOPING YOURSELF

You are entering a new phase of life as a teenager, and it's time to discover new ways to increase and develop your independence. You will naturally begin to increase independence as you grow older, take on more responsibilities, and develop stronger opinions. It feels amazing, but can be hard to balance if you are still living at home. Just know that it is possible and with the right strategies you will be able to gain a new sense of independence.

FINDING INDEPENDENCE

Here are a few ways you can start taking on more responsibilities and increase your independence as a teenager:

Start taking initiative around the house— You are going to need to know how to take care of yourself and a home when you move out or head off to college. By taking on more responsibilities around the house with chores, organization, and cleaning, you will show your parents that you are becoming more independent and teach yourself some valuable skills at the same time. If you are looking for ways to gain the trust of your parents, pitching in a little more and volunteering to help when you weren't asked will be very impressive.

Develop your passions and do things on your own— As you grow and develop you will discover new interests and passions. The best way to explore these and increase your sense of independence is by doing things alone. Maybe you are interested in singing; rather than waiting for a friend to join the choir with you, you can join alone! Doing things on your own can be scary, but it truly is the best way to get to know yourself, take on more responsibility, and gain confidence in yourself and your abilities.

Take your future plans and education seriously— If you are looking for other ways to take your future into your own hands and prove that you are responsible to the people around you, this is a great place to start. Dedicating yourself to your studies, learning more about your desired career, and looking into the options you have for the future are awesome ways to step into your independence.

Find a way to get yourself around— Being able to go places on your own without a parent chauffeuring you around, brings a great sense of freedom. But what if you don't have a car? If you don't have your license, don't have a car, live in a city, or simply want to find alternative methods of transport here are a few other options you have:

- Bicycling— This is a great (and cheap) mode of transport that allows you to get places rather quickly and whenever you need. This is a great option if your city is a welcoming place to cyclers with bike lanes and open roads.
- Public transportation— If the area you live in has a good public transportation system this could be a good way for you to discover more independence and get yourself around. Using public transportation to figure out how to get somewhere by bus or train is also a great way to practice problem-solving skills!
- An electric scooter or moped— If you aren't comfortable with a car, don't have your license, or can't afford one, these are cheaper and easier options you may be able to start using!

Earn your own money— If you can stop depending on your parents for a monthly allowance, start making your own money with a job, and learn to budget early on, you will naturally develop more independence! If you don't want to get a part-time job as an employee, here are a few other side gigs you could pick up to make a bit of extra money:

- Babysitting
- Selling crafts, jewelry, and art online
- Tutoring
- Doing yard work or mowing lawns
- Pet sitting
- Dog walking

Travel whenever possible— Getting out and traveling on your own is an awesome way to gain more independence and develop responsibility. You will first need to start by talking to a parent or school counselor to see which options are available to you. Here are some ways you can get started:

- Join a club that takes trips— Joining a club or team that you are passionate about and traveling with them is a great first step. You might have the chance to travel out of state or across the country with a sports team or the debate team.
- Study abroad and exchange programs— This is a great way for students to get out of their comfort zone in a safe environment for extended periods of time. Going to a new country to study is one of the best ways for young people to find more independence and develop a more diverse worldview.
- Volunteer work— Churches and schools will often take trips to volunteer in other states or countries. If you have volunteered with them in the past or have experience with volunteer work you might have the opportunity to join and make an impact on a new community.
- Language immersion— Similar to study-abroad programs, language immersion programs allow students to travel to a new country to study their native language.

Date responsibly

Your parents might have rules about how early you are allowed to date, and these rules are usually just there to protect you from getting hurt. However, if you and your parents are comfortable with exploring dating, you are being entrusted with a huge responsibility. Here are a few ways you can date in a responsible way, gain independence, and increase trust with your parents:

- Don't let dating affect your school or work ethic— A good partner will not hold you back from reaching your goals and being successful.
- Listen to your parents' rules— You can gain more trust from your parents and date more responsibly by listening to the rules they set for you. This might include a curfew and not closing your bedroom door with you two together. If your parents are always worried about you and your whereabouts, they will stop trusting you with this new independence.
- Keep communication open between you and a trusted adult— There are bad people in this world, and no matter how much you care for someone, there is always a possibility that they could hurt you. If you want to date in a safe way, be sure to keep communication open with an adult you trust. This way you can ask for support, advice, and anything else you may need as you explore the world of dating.

KEYS TO SELF-DEVELOPMENT

A big part of gaining independence and responsibility as a teen is taking steps to improve yourself. If you are able to prove to yourself and your parents that you care about being *better*, you will slowly start to take on more responsibility and gain more freedom. Below are some key habits you can start this week to develop yourself and be more well-rounded!

Actively seek out new activities and passions

Another great way to practice self-development is by actively looking to develop new skills, activities, and passions. You are constantly evolving, and your interests are too. So, don't let the fear of not being perfect stop you— new things are meant to challenge you. The reality is that you will never improve yourself if you don't step out of your comfort zone!

Identifying your strengths and exercising them

In your journal, write out a few things you *know* you are really good at. These could be your best skills, natural talents, or things you have worked hard for. When you are able to recognize what you're good at, it's just a matter of putting energy into those things to develop yourself as a person. Just like muscles need exercise to stay strong, so do your skills!

Independence and self-development can be tricky, but with all of the tools above you now have a sturdy foundation! You've got this!

FINAL WORDS

You have discovered so many new skills and are ready to launch onto the next chapter of your life. Come back here whenever you want reminders, guidance, or to refresh yourself on the tips listed here. Your teenage years are exciting, daunting, and everything in between! So appreciate every second of them!

Image Credit: Shutterstock.com

ALSO BY GRACE DANIELS

Life Skills for Kids

Life Skills for Teenage Boys

Coming Soon:

The Growth Mindset for Teens

The Growth Mindset for Kids

REFERENCES

Eating disorders. AWARE. (2022). Retrieved February 19, 2023, from https://www.aware.org.sg/information/eating-disorders/

Fairfax County Public Schools. (2023). *How to handle peer pressure*. How to Handle Peer Pressure. Retrieved February 16, 2023, from https://www.fcps.edu/student-wellness-tips/peer-pressure

Lyness, D. A. (Ed.). (2018, October). *Body dysmorphic disorder (for teens) - nemours kidshealth*. KidsHealth. Retrieved February 18, 2023, from https://kidshealth.org/en/teens/body-image-problem.html

The Nemours Foundation. (n.d.). *Safety & First Aid (for teens) - nemours kidshealth*. KidsHealth. Retrieved February 19, 2023, from https://kidshealth.org/en/teens/safety/#catfirst-aid

Reynolds, N. (2020, October 12). *10 important social skills you need to teach your teen now*. Raising Teens Today. Retrieved February 17, 2023, from https://raisingteenstoday.com/10-important-social-skills-you-need-to-teach-your-teen-now/

Spence, J. (2021, March 5). *Nonverbal communication: How body language & nonverbal cues are key*. Lifesize. Retrieved February 17, 2023, from https://www.lifesize.com/blog/speaking-without-words/

What are social skills? SkillsYouNeed. (2023). Retrieved February 17, 2023, from https://www.skillsyouneed.com/ips/social-skills.html

Manufactured by Amazon.ca
Acheson, AB